# APRIL 4, 1968

## ALSO BY MICHAEL ERIC DYSON

*Know What I Mean? Reflections on Hip Hop* (2007)

*Debating Race* (2007)

*Pride: The Seven Deadly Sins* (2006)

*Come Hell or High Water:*
*Hurricane Katrina and the Color of Disaster* (2006)

*Is Bill Cosby Right?*
*Or Has the Black Middle Class Lost Its Mind?* (2005)

*Mercy, Mercy Me:*
*The Art, Loves, and Demons of Marvin Gaye* (2004)

*The Michael Eric Dyson Reader* (2004)

*Why I Love Black Women* (2003)

*Open Mike:*
*Reflections on Philosophy, Race, Sex, Culture, and Religion* (2003)

*Holler If You Hear Me: Searching for Tupac Shakur* (2001)

*I May Not Get There with You:*
*The True Martin Luther King, Jr.* (2000)

*Race Rules: Navigating the Color Line* (1996)

*Between God and Gangsta Rap:*
*Bearing Witness to Black Culture* (1996)

*Making Malcolm: The Myth and Meaning of Malcolm X* (1995)

*Reflecting Black: African-American Cultural Criticism* (1993)

# APRIL 4, 1968

## MARTIN LUTHER KING, JR.'S

### DEATH AND

### HOW IT CHANGED

### AMERICA

MICHAEL ERIC

# DYSON

BASIC
CIVITAS
BOOKS

NEW YORK

Books published by Basic Civitas Books are available at special discounts for
bulk purchases in the United States by corporations, institutions, and
other organizations. For more information, please contact the
Special Markets Department at the Perseus Books Group,
2300 Chestnut Street, Suite 200, Philadelphia, PA 19103, or call
(800) 255-1514, or e-mail special.markets@perseusbooks.com.

Design by Jane Raese
Text set in 12-point Garamond 3

Library of Congress Cataloging-in-Publication Data is available for this book.

ISBN-13: 978-0-465-00212-2

2 4 6 8 10 9 7 5 3 1

TO

## MS. OPRAH WINFREY

THE FULFILLMENT OF THE DREAM

WHO LOOKS OUT ON THE PROMISED LAND HE MADE POSSIBLE

# CONTENTS

## PART THREE

## Joshua: Charismatic Black Leadership in a Prophet's Shadow

# PREFACE

When Martin Luther King, Jr., was murdered, I was a nine-year-old schoolboy. I had no idea who he was, had never heard his name or seen him in action. Just as technology had allowed him to speak at his own funeral, it offered me my first glimpse of King's oratorical magic. Like so many folk born after he died, I first met King on television. I was sitting on the living room floor of my inner city Detroit home. "Martin Luther King, Jr., has just been shot in Memphis, Tennessee," the newsman announced, interrupting whatever program we were watching. My father sat behind me in his favorite chair. He was barely able to utter "humph." It was one of those compressed sighs that held back far more pain than it let loose. It came from deep inside his body, an involuntary reflex like somebody had punched him in the gut.

The newsman reported that King had been seriously wounded on a hotel balcony. Then we were ushered by film into Mason Temple for the climax of King's soul shaking last speech. When he finished, I was stunned— that words could thrill me that way, that they could cause such delicious pandemonium in an audience. King's electrifying rhetoric stood the hair on my arms at attention. Soon the newsman broke faith once more with the scheduled programming to announce the final tragedy.

"Martin Luther King, Jr., has been assassinated in Memphis, Tennessee, at thirty-nine years old."

After King's death, I hungered to know him. I haunted libraries in search of biographies, sent off for recordings of his speeches, talked to teachers about his life. I learned that he was a man of peace and love. I also got scared: if King could be murdered for seeking to heal the nation's racial fractures, then all black men might be vulnerable. I thought to myself: "If they killed him, and he didn't want to harm anybody, then they could kill me too." For more than a year, I couldn't stand in front of the upstairs bathroom sink because a door with a window opened onto a small balcony. I feared that I, too, might be taken out. The bullet that shattered King's jaw lodged fragments of fear deep inside my psyche.

*April 4, 1968* is my effort to grapple with King's death—in my own mind, and in the life of the nation. My earlier book on the leader wrestled with his radical legacy and the way it had been hijacked by conservatives out to remake King into an opponent of both affirmative action and a culture that usefully takes race into account. The present study aims to understand just how dominant death was in King's life—how he fought death and faced it down all the same, even as he used death to rally his people in the fight for justice. By probing how King embraced death's inevitability to shape his social agenda, we may better understand how he secured his legacy on the bloody battlefields of racial transformation.

If King was his people's Moses, their charismatic and bold leader, then his vision of the Promised Land has influenced how later generations of black folk have measured their distance from the achievements he foresaw. It has been 40 years since King gave his last will and testament in Memphis and encouraged his followers to believe that he had seen the future promise of fulfillment. Are we any closer to King's beloved community, or are we wandering in a vast racial wilderness from which there is no easy escape? If the signs of arrival into the land of milk and honey are strongest for the wealthiest among us, they are depressing and weak for the poorest. Our faltering quest for justice for the lowliest members of our community suggests the responsibility of the most gifted to forge a path on their behalf. This, after all, is how King spent his last days, fighting for the rights and increased wages of striking sanitation workers. And what of the Joshuas left standing to lead their people into the Promised Land? Has charismatic leadership run its course, or do Messianic leaders still have a role to play in our national destiny? Jesse Jackson, Al Sharpton and Barack Obama all in varying ways can claim aspects of King's black Christian leadership mantle. But have they measured up to King's own vision of how those who would come after him must respond to the crises at hand?

On the 40th anniversary of Martin Luther King, Jr.'s death, it is sobering to realize that he will have been dead longer than he lived. And yet his deeply moving moral vision has lasted beyond the grave. King's painful but productive martyrdom rescued both his failing reputation as a great leader and the efforts of black folk to move further along the path to racial redemption and national thriving. But now that King is enshrined in a national holiday, his challenge to the status quo—and thus his ability as a symbol to inspire radical social change—is smothered beneath banalities and platitudes.

Only by turning to his death and martyrdom can we size up the work that remains to be done and address the suffering and hardship that too many of the folk he loved continue to face. If January 15, 1929, is a holiday celebration trumpeting the arrival of the prophet, then April 4, 1968, is a day that directly confronts the sorrows and death we must forever negotiate. King's memory continues to call us forward out of our creature comforts into the sacrifices of body and spirit that he routinely made. If we hear again his voice, and listen once more to his enduring faith, even as he confronts death, we just might successfully conquer the death and grief in our own souls and in our nation. And we might just resurrect the hope we need to inch even closer to the Promised Land he saw.

*Well I don't know what will happen now. We've got some difficult days ahead. But it really doesn't matter with me now. Because I've been to the mountaintop. And I don't mind. Like anybody, I would like to live a long life. Longevity has its place. But I'm not concerned about that now. I just want to do God's will. And He's allowed me to go up to the mountain. And I've looked over. And I've seen the Promised Land. I may not get there with you. But I want you to know tonight, that we as a people will get to the Promised Land. And so I'm happy tonight. I'm not worried about anything. I'm not fearing any man. "Mine eyes have seen the glory of the coming of the Lord."*

—MARTIN LUTHER KING, JR., APRIL 3, 1968

# PART ONE

# MOSES

## A PROPHET'S DEATH

### IN THREE ACTS

# ACT
# ONE

## FIGHTING DEATH

YOU CANNOT HEAR THE NAME MARTIN
Luther King, Jr., and not think of death. You might hear
the words "I have a dream," but they will doubtlessly only
serve to underscore an image of a simple motel balcony, a
large man made small, a pool of blood. For as famous as he
may have been in life it is, and was, death that ultimately
defined him. Born into a people whose main solace was
Christianity's Promised Land awaiting them after the suffering of this world, King took on the power of his race's
presumed destiny and found in himself the defiance necessary to spark change. He ate, drank, and slept death. He
danced with it, he preached it, he feared it, and he stared
it down. He looked for ways to lay it aside, this burden
of his own mortality, but ultimately knew that his
unwavering insistence on a nonviolent end to the mistreatment of his people could only end violently.

Before anyone ever threatened him, King nearly died by his own hands. As a youth, he tried to kill himself twice because of his love for his grandmother. King's first fling with fate came after an accident. His brother A.D. slid down a banister and knocked their beloved matriarch motionless to the ground. Fearing that his grandmother was dead, King ran upstairs to his room at the back of the house and leaped from the opened window. He got up from his escapade unscathed after he learned that she had survived. The next time trouble struck, neither of them would be so lucky. King snuck away from home to watch a parade in Atlanta's Negro business district. His headiness of getting away with something forbidden and glee at the thrill of seeing a parade were interrupted when a friend told him that he had better hurry home. While he was having his illicit fun, his grandmother had died of a heart attack. King's youthful frolic buried him in guilt, causing him to naively wonder whether God was punishing the family because he had committed the sin of disobedience. Remorse and religion pushed him out of the window a second time. He survived his sophomore spill, but without the consoling presence of one of his biggest boyhood boosters.

The year King was born was the first in over sixty years that the South wasn't soaked in the blood of over a thousand annual lynchings. From the moment the Civil War ended until the day he was born, a theater of intimidation through public death was reenacted across the country, and had nearly codified in King's backyard. His grandparents and parents, his uncles and aunts, every single member of his family before him had learned how to live in fear, how to abide the Jim Crow ways, and how to provide for the next generation a haven carved within a black community of like-minded survivors. It was also a time of deep economic depression, and in the following decade progress would come for the African American community with the New Deal and the WPA. But the forward momentum would also be hounded by the dark forces that had been beaten back by anti-lynching associations, only to find horrific new ways to enact their particular brand of vengeance.

King later confessed that his grandmother's death forced him to clarify his beliefs about the afterlife while causing a crisis of faith. Raised in the home of a respected evangelical minister, King swallowed the beliefs around him without the need to question his father's authority. But with his grandmother went his blind faith, and though his adherence to personal morality never really wavered, a profound skepticism ate away at his fundamentalist core. It prompted him to challenge the bodily resurrection of Jesus in his father's church. King's skepticism persisted; by the second year of college he regretted going to church. He eventually cast off the narrowness of his father's church and found his own solace in a far more liberal interpretation of Christianity, pursuing truth in theology and philosophy, always seeking answers from whatever source lay at hand. His questioning nature later served him well as a leader who was open to new ideas. This piercing style of intellectual debate proved a boon to his staff, as they relished the lively and contentious interactions that King encouraged.

If King escaped his boyhood fundamentalism, he couldn't shake the foreboding finger of death that traced across his life. From the time he began to speak out, King was haunted by death—mugged by the promise of destruction for seeking an end to black indignity and the beginning of equality with whites. After a few years spent up North acquiring his education, King chose to return to where he would be needed most in the coming years—the white-hot center of the burgeoning civil rights movement and Montgomery, Alabama. At twenty-six he took on the responsibilities of a Baptist pulpit, joining forces with the local NAACP, and dug in for the yearlong bus boycott created to end the Jim Crow law of racial segregation in public transportation. During this conflict his house was bombed—his wife, Coretta, and their ten-week-old daughter, Yolanda, were home but escaped injury. It was the first time King would be tested with violence aimed at his life, but far from the last. Later in the boycott a shotgun blast was fired into King's home. King did not capitulate, but instead he emerged from the ashes of these attempts as the true phoenix of the newly minted movement. Once again, his mortality challenged, he accepted his calling without hesitation.

A couple of years after the boycott ended, King was in Harlem at Blumstein's Department Store signing *Stride Toward Freedom*, his account of the movement's success. From out of nowhere, a clearly disturbed black woman, Izola Ware Curry, sunk a letter opener into his chest after asking if he was Martin Luther King. Though considered an act of instability, this attack was still colored by Curry's irrational hatred of what King and the NAACP were trying to do, and by her own fear of being killed because of his constant stirring of the pot. Even so, it was one of the rare instances of black public hate directed at King, the kind that would later be famously associated with his colleague and competitor Malcolm X.

As he took flight to snip the bullying wings of Jim Crow, King ruffled the feathers of white racists, who grew more determined to bring him down. There was striking physical intimidation of King. In a show of naked aggression, two white cops attempted to block his entry into a Montgomery courtroom for the trial of a man who had attacked King's comrade Ralph Abernathy. Despite a warning from the cops, King poked his head inside the courtroom looking for his lawyer to help him get inside. His actions ignited their rage. The policemen twisted his arm behind his back and manhandled him into jail. King said the cops "tried to break my arm; they grabbed my collar and tried to choke me, and when they got me to the cell, they kicked me in." A photographer captured the scene. The shot of King—dressed in a natty tan suit, stylish gold wristwatch and a trendy snap-brim fedora—wincing as he was banished to confinement is an iconic civil rights image.

As King addressed the 1962 convention of his organization, the Southern Christian Leadership Conference (SCLC), a two-hundred-pound young white man rushed the stage and landed a brutal blow on his left cheek. The crowd reacted in hushed disbelief. The diminutive King never flinched or retreated, even as the young brute delivered several more blows, first to the side of his face as he stood behind King, and then two blows to his back. King gently spoke to his attacker as he continued to pummel his body. As he was being knocked backward King dropped his hands—legendary activist Septima Clark, in attendance that day, said King let down his hands "like a newborn baby"—and faced his assailant head on.

Finally, SCLC staff leader Wyatt Tee Walker and others intervened as King pleaded, "Don't touch him! Don't touch him. We have to pray for him." King quietly assured the young man he wouldn't be harmed. The leader and his aides retreated to a private office to talk with his assailant, who was, King told the audience when he returned, a member of the American Nazi Party. As King held an ice-filled handkerchief to his jaw, he informed the crowd he wouldn't press charges. Most in attendance were amazed at King's calm as violence flashed. Obviously nonviolence was more than a method and a creed; it answered assault with acts of steadfast courage.

If King was unfazed by battering, he managed, through a Herculean work ethic and a laserlike attention to his purpose, to ride the crushing stream of daily death threats that flowed from Montgomery to Memphis. Everywhere he went, disenfranchised throngs clamored to see him—while hordes of bigots wanted to see him dead. Many of the planes he rode on were delayed because of bomb threats. Many of the buildings he spoke in were secured because of threats of destruction. Many of the speeches he gave at hotels and colleges were delivered knowing that some potential crackpot—or crack shot—was roaming and ready to do him in. Many of the marches he led drew goons who violently complained of the decay of their "pure" white America. And many of the demonstrations he conducted were met by grieving white nationalists full of murderous resentment. King slashed the gnarled, Cro-Magnon verities of white supremacy with his silver tongue. The love-drunk orator also troubled racists by calling on white liberal divines in his pleas for freedom.

King deflected the blows of mortality through rhetoric and philosophy that owed as much to theater as to theology. He grasped the benefit of dramatizing his fight with death—and hence, his people's fight with social death as victims of oppression. When King's house was bombed during the boycott in Montgomery, he rushed home from a mass meeting to greet an angry crowd of blacks. By a single dramatic gesture—holding up his hand to silence the crowd, just as Malcolm X would later wave his hand over an angry crowd of Muslims in Harlem to retreat, causing a white policeman to say, "That's too much power for one man to have"—King reassured them that his wife and baby were safe. He asked them not to panic or resort to violence. "If you have weapons, take them home. He who lives by the sword will perish by the sword. Remember that is what Jesus said. We are not advocating violence. We want to love our enemies."

King urged his listeners to believe in the moral beauty of their fight for justice. Death could not derail such a movement. "I want it to be known the length and breadth of this land that if I am stopped, this movement will not stop. If I am stopped, our work will not stop. For what we are doing is right, what we are doing is just," King declared. "If anything happens to me, there will be others to take my place." It was a shrewd appeal to his listeners' religious beliefs. He also reinforced the virtues of non-violence and underscored his humility as a leader. And he situated, and thereby downplayed the effect of, his possible death in a broader movement that was impossible to stop. It was the perfect fusion of truth and art.

To be sure, King was courageous in the face of death. But he confessed to his audiences that he was often afraid as well. He inspired his listeners to swap their fears for faith, just as he had done. "I went to bed many nights scared to death," King admitted, referring to the early days of the boycott. Death threats were frequent. After one of them, King got a new dose of faith in a famous kitchen encounter with God. That experience led him to an adult belief in a personal deity. King says he heard a voice saying to him to "'preach the gospel, stand up for truth, stand up for righteousness.' Since that morning I can stand up without fear." That didn't mean there weren't relapses and new struggles to overcome, or reaffirmations of faith to be made.

In a mass meeting after city buses were integrated, King voiced the sorrow and fear of black Montgomery over violent white backlash. King was toiling under the increased pressures of a man who had become a symbol for his people. He also faced the jealousy of fellow activists because of the ink and spotlight that followed him. So King took to the pulpit to pray for God's guidance. He sowed a few phrases that reaped a harvest of turmoil in his audience: "Lord, I hope no one will have to die as a result of our struggle for freedom in Montgomery. Certainly I don't want to die. But if anyone has to die, let it be me!" King's words were met by a chorus of "No"s that ripped through the congregation. Overcome with emotion, King couldn't continue. He broke down and was led to his seat by two preachers. It was one of the few times that the trauma King routinely endured slipped into public view.

King struggled constantly between bravery and the specter of breakdown. His public proclamations of fearlessness were both truthful and strategic. They were aimed at reinforcing troops in the racial trenches. But in private, blue moods sometimes sucked his spirit dry. There were times when King was undaunted by the prospect of death, addressing it with fairly objective calculation. At other times he was ambushed by the fear and world-weariness known only to those who've been fiendishly chased by government officials, fellow citizens, and hate groups. This didn't make King a hypocrite or a coward. His brutal honesty about death made him bravely human. King warred against death's sovereignty, and in some desperate moments, conceded its ugly ubiquity. In the midst of the battle, he remained strangely hopeful about using death to jumpstart social progress.

There's little doubt that King knew the price he might have to pay if he gave in to the pressures and fortunes of history. Black life was dangerous during the reign of white terror in the fifties. As King was first putting on his robes to preach in Alabama, the Supreme Court was lighting a match with their decision against segregation in *Brown v. Board of Education*. Over the summer of 1955, as the first school year that would see mixed classes approached, the Mississippi Delta began to smolder. On May 7, a black minister—Willie George Washington Lee, the first black person to vote in Humphreys County—was shot in the face, ultimately dying from his wounds. No one was charged, as the local sheriff claimed the buckshots found in his jawbone were probably fillings. On August 13, a sixty-three-year-old farmer and WWII veteran named Lamar Smith was shot on the courthouse lawn in Brookhaven, in front of the sheriff. Three men were arrested, but a grand jury of their white supremacist peers brought no indictments. Later that month a young black teenager would allegedly wolf-whistle at a white woman, and the sparks that had been flying around the state of Mississippi would ignite into one of the most horrendous and infamous lynchings of the twentieth century. Black leadership was even more a risk of one's life for the precious goal of freedom. There were those who coveted leadership in order to profit from the goodies that fell along the lime-lit path of fame. Few were truly willing to sacrifice life and limb to secure rights and privileges for the masses. King zealously embraced the task, and by doing so, inspired other leaders to do the same. "If a man hasn't found something he's willing to die for," King was fond of repeating, "he isn't fit to live." When a reporter asked him if he was afraid after a spasm of violence in Montgomery, King demurred. "Once you become dedicated to a cause, personal security is not the goal. It is greater than that. What will happen to you personally does not matter. My cause, my race, is worth dying for."

King refined his argument in an essay, writing: "If physical death is the price that a man must pay to free his children and his white brethren from a permanent death of the spirit, then nothing could be more redemptive." In an interview with Alex Haley in *Playboy* magazine he further stated: "If I were constantly worried about death, I couldn't function. After a while, if your life is more or less constantly in peril, you come to a point where you accept the possibility philosophically." Saying that all leaders must face the fact that "America today is an extremely sick nation" and that "something could happen to me at any time," King concluded that "my cause is so right, so moral, that if I should lose my life, in some way it would aid the cause."

Regardless of these brave assertions, it would be a mistake to conclude that King was cavalier about death. Even as he acknowledged the strong possibility he might die, King fought death to the end. Less than two weeks before he was shot down, King joked with an audience in Albany, Georgia, that he had to "pray [his chartered plane] all the way in" because for a long while the plane's engine wouldn't start, making the leader late for his speech. "Now, as I've often said, I don't want to give the impression that I don't have faith in God in the air; it's simply that I've had more experience with him on the ground." At a press conference in Los Angeles after Malcolm X's death in 1965, King disclosed a discussion he had with Attorney General Katzenbach about his own safety. King admitted that death threats "are not too pleasant to discuss so I didn't want to go into great detail."

When a reporter quizzed him about the potential violence that would result from his death, King began his answer by declaring, "Well, I certainly hope that nothing happens to me." In a speech delivered at Los Angeles' Victory Baptist Church under death threats, King said: "I don't ever request police protection, but when it's given

14

I don't ever turn it down . . . I wish I could take them back with me to Selma." King was scheduled to leave California for Selma to lead the campaign for voting rights, where he faced several more credible death threats. Before he left, King placed calls to several go-betweens to recruit prominent citizens to telegram President Johnson and seek federal protection for the leader. The brutality and murder that marchers later faced in Selma warranted King's request. On occasion, King balked at going places where the threat of death loomed, only to face down his fears and troop on.

King courageously resisted the forces that caucused against him. But the unrelenting threat of bombs exploding and snipers shooting took its toll. King suffered desperate stretches of depression that sometimes alarmed his closest aides and friends. He fought valiantly to maintain sanity and focus as his body rebelled against the baleful disharmonies of white supremacy. One of his top aides wanted him to consult a psychiatrist because of his steep descent into the doldrums. The sleeping pills he got from a physician friend stopped working. King's reliance on elbow-bending to combat insomnia and exhaustion dramatically increased. His vacations rarely allowed him to escape his troubles and pressures. And the somber tones of his voice evoked the nightmares that stalked him when he wakened from unsatisfying sleep. Martin Luther King was a marked man. There was little possibility of retreat from the maelstrom that called his name and sought his blood.

Is it little wonder that King's philosophical armor sometimes wore thin in the ghastly confrontation with his own mortality? The inhuman pace of his schedule alone was enough to wear out five men. But the energy it took to grapple with death-dealing, death-denying, death-delaying, death-avoiding, and death-embracing could only last so long. King shuttled theologically between Jesus's confident stoicism in the face of death—"Now is my soul troubled; and what shall I say? Father, save me from this hour: but for this cause came I unto this hour"—and his wrenching desire in Gethsemane to slip the burden of saving the world through his own bloodshed: "O my Father, if it be possible, let this cup pass from me." If Jesus could be torn between cosmic obligation and existential terror, it makes sense that the same could be true for his ebony disciple.

Still, it is nearly miraculous that King managed to keep death in a philosophical headlock as often as he did. Sure, he sometimes cried uncle in private and was bulldozed by impenetrable despondency. But King rallied to declare in public what he knew to be true, both *despite* and *because* of his suffering. King's plight made this clear: If sleep is the cousin of death, then depression is its little brother. His depressions often felt like death only slightly delayed. King's public dreams and private nightmares formed the raw and the cooked of his civil rights world. His dreams were the natural reflex of hope and redeemed curiosity. His depressions were largely the result of the social evils he encountered. Despite the despair that tempted him, King promoted hope and curiosity to his dying day.

King's hope flashed even as he said that the nation's political drift led to spiritual death. If he had given up on the American dream he would have stopped being disappointed in white America. King's bitter indictment of the country's unconscious racism grew from his lover's quarrel with America. He said that unfair white privileges had to die for black equality to be born. King made an even more striking argument: that black moral discipline could redeem a decaying white America. King was fond of quoting historian Arnold Toynbee's claim that "it may be the Negro who will give the spiritual dynamic to Western civilization that it so desperately needs to survive."

But helping to save Western civilization came at a cost: even a superior black morality wasn't enough to rescue the nation. Black blood would have to flow to complete the task. King never tired of telling black folk that unearned suffering, even death, is redemptive. King spoke of how he and, by extension, his followers, could transform "suffering into a creative force . . . Recognizing the necessity for suffering I have tried to make it a virtue . . . I have attempted to see my personal ordeals as an opportunity to transform myself and heal the people involved in the tragic situation which now obtains. I have lived these last few years with the conviction that unearned suffering is redemptive." The logic is clear: since suffering, including death, can't be avoided, turn it to advantage and wrest from evil a sweet and ironic victory. Nobody did that better than King.

King made a virtue of necessity by brilliantly using death—the threat of it, the use of it to terrorize black folk, the fact of its existence to spoil the black quest for justice—as a means to inspire black folk to keep going, and to signal to white racists that their way wouldn't win. King presided over the spectacle of black death with stirring imagination. He cast light on the harsh interior of black mortality and found a costly but triumphant immortality as its reward. The threat and reality of death played many roles simultaneously: It was a bitter arena to be played. It was also the producer, director, and often the co-star of many civil rights performances—marches, demonstrations, funerals, rallies, protests, freedom rides, sit-ins, speeches, and eulogies. No one presided over the theater of death with more skill than King. No one brought as much drama and passion to the play of death and life as King.

And no one directed the response of black folk in the face of death with as much brilliance and cunning, or as much courage and brio, as King. In thousands of speeches, eulogies, pep talks, sermons, essays, articles, and books, King rehearsed the use and consequence of death. He re-hearsed it too, placing death into convenient moral coffins after he publicly slayed the fear of death in axiom and anecdote. King got pugilistic about the fear of death. He boxed his way across the canvass of American moral and social life, tagging the fiercest enemy of black progress with rhetorical uppercuts and verbal jabs.

King also waged war against death and the anxieties it birthed by finding bright purpose behind its ominous clouds. At the funeral for three of the four little girls blown to glory in a Birmingham church bombing—Addie Mae Collins, Carol Denise McNair, and Cynthia Diane Wesley—King argued that their deaths "say to us that we must be concerned not merely about who murdered them, but about the system, the way of life, the philosophy which produced the murderers. Their death says to us that we must work passionately and unrelentingly for the realization of the American dream." King also insisted that the little girls' deaths could force a greater good if we would heed the lessons of their murder. King argued that only the redeeming action of the girls' survivors—all citizens of good will—could defy the logic, and deny the victory, of the hateful murderers who nipped the sweet flower of their lives in the bud. And he linked their deaths to the transformation of the broader society. "And so my friends, they did not die in vain. God still has a way of wringing good out of evil. And history has proven over and over again that unmerited suffering is redemptive. The innocent blood of these little girls may well serve as a redemptive force that will bring new light to this dark city."

King creatively contested death's dreary, thudding, throbbing persistence. At times, he sought to trump its existential agony through philosophical detachment, and a near clinical exposure of its pathologies and pitfalls. At other times, he narrated its approach, first in his own skin, then glimpsing it rattling the roost of neighbors in the vicinity of fear. King knew intimately of death's sneaky approach, how it could trade vulgar visibility for tacit implosions, such as a nagging insecurity that robbed the Negro of confidence. King tirelessly detested the "clouds of inferiority in the mental skies" of black folk.

He also discerned the disparagement of blackness that took root in the language of social analysis and cultural criticism before it flowered in black self-hate. Inspired by Ossie Davis, King frequently cited the 60 negative synonyms for blackness of the 120 contained in *Roget's Thesaurus*. By comparison, whiteness was given a clean bill among its 134 synonyms. It was black death by other means, a calculated and systematic deprivation of Negro self-worth that drew from the poisoned wells of bigotry. And neither was the battle merely academic to King. He protested, half jokingly, as the black movement turned north and began to focus on rehabilitating the black self-image, that he was black and beautiful, and that he had good hair too, a nod to the growing defeat in the black psyche of white styles of beauty—including black folks' desperate elevation of fairer skin and straighter hair, neither of which King possessed.

If King took these psychological contests to heart, he couldn't help but make the battle against death a personal one as well. At times, King sought outlets for his depression and fear in gallows humor. After preaching at the funeral of Alabama activist Jimmie Lee Jackson (a black Vietnam veteran who was shot by state troopers at a voter's rights rally for intervening in the beating of his mother and grandfather) and leading a procession to Jackson's gravesite, King flagged SCLC board member Joseph Lowery. "Come, walk with me, Joe," King said. "This may be my last walk." King and his comrades often preached mock funerals for one another to cut the tension. However, it was Jackson's brutal and wrongful death that helped spark the Selma to Montgomery march. King's depression only deepened, from fatigue and exhaustion, as well as the ever-present nag of death. Peace was being met with violence regardless of how hard he prayed or preached. He turned to food and alcohol for comfort; he gained weight but no relief from his raw nerves. A former staff member for Summer Community Organization and Political Education (SCOPE) said that King "was depressed," that he "was dark, gaunt and tired," that he "felt that his time was up . . . He said that he knew they were going to get him."

Every eulogy King delivered undoubtedly made him think of the words that would be said over him. Every death he observed made him think of his own death. When John F. Kennedy was assassinated in Dallas, Texas, he had said to his wife, Coretta, "This is what is going to happen to me also. I keep telling you, this is a sick society." It is easy to gauge the loneliness King must have felt in Coretta's response. "I was not able to say anything. I had no word to comfort my husband. I could not say, 'It won't happen to you.' I felt he was right. It was a painfully agonizing silence. I moved closer to him and gripped his hand in mine." Even when consolations were offered, King deflected them. After a plane King boarded received a bomb threat in 1964, he told his wife and aide Dorothy Cotton that "I've told you all that I don't expect to survive this revolution; this society's too sick." After Cotton tried to reassure him, King replied, "Well, I'm just being realistic." And whatever differences the two leaders may have had, Malcolm X's brutal gunning-down in 1965 must have shattered many a restless sleep for King thereafter.

King's friend Deenie Drew said that in his "last year or so, I had a feeling that Martin had a death wish . . . I had a feeling that he didn't know which way to turn." King was so preoccupied with his own death, so obsessed with its likely occurrence, that in the last years he could only relax in a room with no windows because he was tortured with worry about who might pull the trigger. His eyes fell on strangers, wondering if they were the messenger of death. King asked former aide Bayard Rustin, "You think I'm paranoid, don't you?" referring to the brooding monopoly of death in his mind. Rustin confessed he did. Increasingly marginalized in his own pain, as there were very few people to whom he could confide the depths of his obsession, King suffered huge grief of soul and heart, largely alone.

# ACT
# TWO

## TALKING DEATH

THE DEEPER MARTIN LUTHER KING, JR., sank into a private hell of unquenchable bleakness, the higher he rose in pulpits and rostrums across the nation to preach the fear from his own breast, and those of his fellow strivers. Just as he gave most of his pocketbook and preaching to the movement, King offered up his despondency as well. King channeled his deflation and demoralization into the searing oratory that would form his *automortology*, a genre of speech that looked past his death to tell the story of how he should be viewed once his life was over. Automortology looks back on a self whose past lies in the future. Automortology, at least on King's tongue, rolled off in a tense that might be called the *future moral anterior*, what will and should have been true about his life and death. King took revenge on his death before it occurred—a linguistic vengeance that was the only possible one he could take as an advocate of nonviolence. This was a case of "If you can't beat them, then you can beat them to it," as King made first claim to interpreting his life after his own lights. Judging by the sermons and speeches he gave, it was a bitterly pleasurable exorcism of vexing spirits.

"Every now and then I guess we all think realistically about that day when we will be victimized with what is life's final common denominator—that something that we call death," King declared in his home pulpit of Ebenezer Baptist Church in Atlanta exactly two months before his assassination. "We all think about it."

These words appear at the close of "The Drum Major Instinct," a homily made famous after excerpts of it were played at King's nationally televised funeral. The point of King's sermon was to unmask the yearning "to be important, to surpass others . . . to lead the parade," calling it the "drum major instinct" after psychoanalyst Alfred Adler, who argued that "this quest for recognition, this desire for attention, this desire for distinction is the basic impulse." King argued that the hunger for recognition and praise is understandable; it may even be a healthy boost to the ego. Still, the "drum major instinct" often tempted individuals to snobbish behavior and drove nations to war to prove their dominance. It may seem odd for King to discuss his death in such a sermon. But the meaning comes clear when he ties reflections on his mortality to the kind of instincts he'd like to be remembered for championing.

King briefly discusses death in a general, philosophical way, staking his claim in the subject as an analyst interested in its psychological fallout. But his abbreviated discourse on death quickly gets personal. After all, sermons are not exercises in objective inquiry as much as intellectually and emotionally charged speech meant to persuade hearers of the gospel's truth. Eyewitness—better yet, "I" witness—gives testimony a prized place in black sacred talk. It's great to know what Isaiah or Jeremiah said, and nice to hear what Aristotle or Du Bois thought, but "what say *ye*" is the biblical archaism that resounds in black sanctuaries.

King swiftly moves from the universal, "We all think about it," to the particular, and from psychology to automortology, as he confesses, "And every now and then I think about my own death and I think about my own funeral." To be sure, death flows constantly through the black Christian universe, with its cycle of grief and consolation released in funerals, eulogies, burials, gravesite visits, and memorial services. But like most religious communities, death is ritually segregated: beyond special sermons, constant but sprinkled pulpit references, prayer-meeting soliloquies, or as an adjunct to the preacher's perpetual inducement to sinners to get right with God before it's too late, the subject is usually taken up with sustained seriousness at funerals. And speaking extensively of one's own death in first person singular leapfrogged way past the call for personal testimony in most black churches. What most of King's parishioners had no way of knowing is that his mood was increasingly funereal, though he quickly protested the thought that he was in any way morose about the subject. Listening to King's voice, bathed in weary sadness and dripping in pathos, it's hard to miss the heartbreak just beneath the sermonic surface.

"And I don't think of it in a morbid sense. And every now and then I ask myself, 'What is it that I would want said?' And I leave the word to you this morning." King was explicit and sincere, if completely unrealistic, in his wishes: a short funeral, a brief eulogy, no mention of his Nobel Peace Prize or his hundreds of other awards, and no mention of where he attended school. Instead, King wanted his eulogist to say that he served and loved others, that he tried to be "right on the war question," that he tried to "feed the hungry, clothe the naked, and visit the imprisoned," and then, as if to recap the point, that he "tried to love and serve humanity."

King concludes by saying that should his eulogist call him a drum major, it should honor his dominant quest for justice, peace, and righteousness. King said, "I won't have any money to leave behind. I won't have the fine and luxurious things of life to leave behind. But I just want to leave a committed life behind." He confessed the desire to be at Jesus' side—the same way that James and John, the protagonists of the biblical story he hung his sermon on, wanted to be there, except in their case it was for personal glory and political advantage. King wanted to be near his Lord to play the role of servant that he claimed in his sermon was the true mark of greatness. "I just want to be there in love and in justice and in truth and in commitment to others, so that we can make of this old world a new world."

King's automortology permits him to strike a solemn blow against death by delivering his eulogy in advance of the event. He wins, temporarily at least, the battle to publicly declare his death, even if it was a fictional projection of the end. In retrospect, that might seem a Pyrrhic victory: King may have furnished his death room in his mind, but it didn't keep his enemies from plotting to lay him in the casket in the flesh. The advantage King got was one of perspective and interpretation. He would dance his way through the land mines of literal, and apparently imminent, termination. And by supplying the narrative that would accompany his corpse, he would be resurrected from the grave his enemies dug for him and enjoy the sort of immortality that he felt was fit for a king. Immortality had nothing to do with man-made toys and earthly bonuses. Instead, immortality was gained in service to the lowly and lost, the heartbroken and despairing, the prisoner and soldier, the hungry and naked, the mass of humanity.

Thus, when the actual date *would* arrive, and the certificate of death *would be* signed, his enemies' act of murder would only confirm King's standing as the very thing they tried to deny—a man who was first among men because he was willing to lose his life in service. What his enemies didn't realize, and what King fought desperately to believe, is that he was in a failsafe position: the more spite they spit, the more opposition they mounted, the more King was pushed to greatness in serving his people. In a strange way, King's life was tied to his enemies in inverse proportion to their attacking, and ultimately, killing him: The more they got their way, the more King got his. King's despondency and death wish could only be defeated by the committed life that he saw himself leaving behind.

Neither should one miss the irony that the miracle of technology permitted King's words to be played at his well-watched funeral, providing a hugely influential venue to air his automortological thoughts and help bring them to pass. He shaped the interpretation of his life in a eulogy of his own words in the aftermath of his death. The same technology also permitted King to say at his funeral what he didn't want said at his funeral. Achieving more than intriguing tautology—after all, there were several eulogies offered—the airing of King's words in effect made him dishonor his own wish of remaining silent about his earthly accomplishments. But his own words may have been the most memorable spoken about him that day.

# I HAVE BEEN TO THE MOUNTAINTOP

The pressures and worries that King endured in his last years stormed him as he delivered what turned out to be his last will and testament. King's "Promised Land" speech in Memphis the night before he was murdered has become perhaps the clearest example of his automortological art, and a heartbreaking work of dialectical genius. King's speech eloquently protested death's arbitrary force. One of automortology's benefits is a sense of control over the story of one's death, even though it may prove a largely illusory control when stacked up against other forces vying to interpret one's death, and hence, one's life—and further still, one's life after death; that is, one's posthumous reputation. But the consolation prize to such competition is that automortology tries to shape the future of one's not-yet past before it is brought to pass. In King's case, the tension between the not-yet and the will-have-been kept intruding on his mind, and in Memphis, he let it flow in his by-then-trademark mellifluous melancholia.

The conditions of King's return visit to Memphis make it remarkable that the speech got delivered at all. His reputation as a nonviolent leader was on the line: a march he led in the city the week before in support of striking sanitation workers had for the first time turned violent from within his crowd. The march was sabotaged by a volatile mix of government-paid rabble-rousers and the short fuses of fatigued forces on the fringe of the black freedom movement. The minor riot that unfurled under King's watch wounded his ego and caught him in the throes of an even deeper depression. He was determined to redo the march and restore the movement's reputation of peaceful means of protest. But to do this he would have to go to court to clear the way. His detractors lay in wait for him, and his closest supporters urged him to move on—they needed his diminished energy focused on the poor people's march on Washington being planned for the end of April. Most of his staff was bitterly opposed to that march too. King was foremost battling crushing exhaustion and the sort of illness he always suffered when his spirits were way down.

When he arrived in Memphis in pouring rain and tornado threats, King took shelter in the Lorraine Motel and sent Ralph Abernathy to speak in his stead at a rally at Mason Temple. King felt the severe weather would scatter his flock, and thus offer opportunity to the press and his enemies to trumpet his declining popularity and influence. Plus, one of the few vanities he clung to as the nation's most celebrated black leader was the right to duck small crowds. Abernathy was Tonto to King's Lone Ranger, the two of them a diminutive tandem galloping into troubled towns, even going to jail together. Abernathy was also Ed McMahon to King's Johnny Carson, warming up the audiences King spoke to with folksy humor and preacherly wit, and sometimes relinquishing his role as second banana to be the big tomato. He could tell when King's absence could be tolerated, and when it would dishearten the audience and the speaker who tried to fill his shoes. When Abernathy stepped into the auditorium, saw the size of the crowd gathered, and felt the letdown of King's missing profile, he rang his sometime roommate and insisted King rise and meet the throng who'd come to see *him*. King dressed and rushed to an audience whose restless energy ultimately lifted his spirits above the thunder and lightning.

In his familiar role of hype man, Abernathy reveled that night in introducing King, speaking uncharacteristically long, more than half an hour, loving his best friend out loud for him and the world to hear. Looking back, Abernathy's gesture gleamed with the same premonition that glowed in King's words—it wasn't hard to discern premonition in a man who faced death threats nearly everywhere he went. As his comrade Andrew Young said, "He always knew some speech would be his last." And even though King asked Abernathy to give the major speech that night while he simply made a few remarks, Abernathy's lavish sentiments roused in King a fiercely articulated and powerfully delivered speech.

Without a note in front of him, King opened by thanking Abernathy, "the best friend that I have in the world." His voice ragged and nearly slurred-sounding at first, there was no indication of the rousing twenty minutes to come. After then thanking his audience for coming despite a storm warning, signs of which battered the building and sliced through his speech as natural sound effects to punctuate his points, King took an imaginative tour of history. Automortology egged King on to turn time against itself and embrace a death whose future had slipped into history. Before he took that leap for the last time, King skirted temporality altogether and stood with God at the beginning of time. In King's imagined survey of history, the Almighty spoke to him by name. King, in turn, spoke of his relationship with God in the same matter-of-fact way that he announced his friendship with Abernathy, or the weather conditions that night. This took what the old folk in black churches often say about being "on speaking terms with God" to a loftier level. Whether he meant to or not, King implied that his credential as a prophet came straight from headquarters. Without such prophetic confidence, any seer is lost from the start.

King thrilled the audience on his sweep through history with a poet's tongue and a philosopher's erudition. After God asked him what period he wanted to live in, King took a "mental flight" over Egypt's Red Sea, and then on to Greece's Mount Olympus, where he would "see Plato, Aristotle, Socrates, Euripides and Aristophanes assembled around the Parthenon as they discussed the great and eternal issues of reality." He'd pass over the Roman Empire, and take a gander at the Renaissance to "get a quick picture" of its contribution to "the cultural and esthetic life of man." King would visit "the man for whom I'm named," Martin Luther, to see him start the Reformation, and then make his way to 1863 "and watch a vacillating president by the name of Abraham Lincoln finally come to the conclusion that he had to sign the Emancipation Proclamation." He'd visit another president who in the early thirties grappled with "the bankruptcy of his nation" and uttered "an eloquent cry that 'we have nothing to fear but fear itself.'" King said he wouldn't stop at any of these places, but instead, would "turn to the Almighty, and say, 'If you allow me to live just a few years in the second half of the twentieth century, I will be happy.'"

King's fictional flight, in search of the best period to live in, lands right in his backyard. That's no surprise to those familiar with a speaker rigging the rhetoric to make necessity a virtue: since you have no choice but to live in the era in which you're born, why not say that, if given the choice, you'd choose that era to live in. It also cuts down on epoch-envy, the lust to live in another time, in greener temporal pastures. It gives your audience a sense that they, too, aren't living in such a bad time, and offers hope to those who think their period is of little use to history or God. King manages the feat nicely, but without insulting his audience's intelligence. He admits that it might seem strange to choose their era to live in, "because the world is all messed up." But he sees "God working in this period of the twentieth century in a way that men, in some strange way, are responding." The masses are rising up, and people around the world are saying, "We want to be free." The human rights revolution is a principal reason King is glad to be alive in his day.

Assured that his audience is happy to be born to their epoch, King challenges them to make the most of their historical advantage by siding with the poor and disenfranchised, determined to throw off their shackles. The black sanitation workers who are on strike are, of course, a centerpiece of King's social homily, but their plight is a test of the nation's commitment to justice. King calls on his audience to identify with the slaves of the Exodus story (the sanitation workers and their allies) who were brutalized in Egypt, pleading that they not be hoodwinked by the divide-and-conquer strategies of "Pharaoh" (Memphis's mayor) and instead unite under the banner of resistance to injustice. It is one of the biblical threads and existing narratives stitched throughout the speech.

Another narrative and theme drawn from the holy book weaves in the Good Samaritan story. King presses the crowd to adopt the "dangerous unselfishness" of the story's protagonist who risked his life to help his fellow man. King wanted the audience to do the same with the sanitation workers. King here employs a modified form of chiasmus, where two clauses are related to each other by reversing their structure to make a bigger point, when he contrasts the Levite who left the stranger by the roadside and the Good Samaritan who aided him: "And so the first question that the Levite asked was, 'If I stop to help this man, what will happen to me?'" But then the Good Samaritan came by. And King reverses the question: "'If I do not stop to help this man, what will happen to him?'" King makes a finer point by also identifying with the two who passed the fallen man on the road, citing the potential for violence on such a meandering and unwelcome road. The Samaritan stopped. King stopped.

King's performance, like that of a jazz musician, improvises on themes of justice, riffs on themes of love, and wails on harsh forces of oppression. King brilliantly moves between the social world of his hearers and the biblical stories they are familiar with to reinforce the moral meaning of their struggle. He also skillfully probes the contours of death. Like all great rhetoricians and jazz musicians, King states and restates his themes, here more quietly, there with more verve and gusto, enlarging his point by repeating it with different examples.

King turns again to his gratitude to God for allowing him to live in the latter part of the twentieth century, and for allowing him to join the sanitation workers in their struggle for dignity, manhood, and fair wages. He underscores his gratitude by imagining how things might have been had he not been around, had he died. King uses automortology to open a historical window onto his role as actor and observer in the civil rights drama. King tells the affecting story of a letter he received after he was stabbed and nearly killed by Izola Ware Curry. With an impeccable sense of timing, King recounts all the letters and telegrams he received in the hospital from dignitaries, including the president, vice president, and governor of New York, whose content he forgot.

But one letter stood out. It was from a writer who'd read that the blade that punctured King's chest rested at the tip of his aorta, and with a single sneeze, he could drown in his own blood. King recalled its content verbatim. "I'll never forget it. It said simply, 'Dear Dr. King: I am a ninth-grade student at the Whites Plains High School.' She said, 'While it should not matter, I would like to mention that I am a white girl. I read in the paper of your misfortune, and of your suffering. And I read that if you had sneezed, you would have died. And I'm simply writing you to say that I'm so happy that you didn't sneeze.'"

Before he can even season the story, let it stew in its juices, cook it and tear off a piece for himself, and then savor it in his mouth before serving the rest to others, the audience, including a great many preachers, belches in emotional response. They know that a gifted wordsmith like King will tease the anecdote to a delicious conclusion. Their anticipation fuels King's hunger to meet their expectations.

"And I want to say tonight, I want to say that I am happy that I didn't sneeze. Because if I had sneezed, I wouldn't have been around here in 1960, when students all over the South started sitting-in at lunch counters."

As the applause and verbal affirmation build, King repeats the phrase. Having visited Greek civilization on his imaginary tour, King again pays homage to their rhetorical invention in the structure of his speech. Anaphora is the Greek term for emphasizing words or phrases by repeating them at the beginning of neighboring clauses. King plays the satisfying, pleasurable repetition to maximum effect, repeating "If I had sneezed" to suggest all the ways he and his colleagues were present and accounted for in racial and democratic revolution. If King had sneezed, he wouldn't have seen the sit-ins, the Albany movement, or the colossal struggle in Birmingham; he wouldn't have dreamed before the Lincoln Memorial, or marched in the Selma campaign. And of course, he "wouldn't have been in Memphis to see a community rally around those brothers and sisters who are suffering. I'm so happy that I didn't sneeze."

In one brilliant gesture, King fuses a variation of automortology and history: he links his death that might have occurred to events that he would have missed. And though he doesn't say it, or even imply it, we're left to wonder if most of those events would have occurred in quite the same way without his presence. Besides identifying with the movement in Memphis, and identifying the movement of history with the strikers, King identifies with the little white girl whose phrase he samples, and then owns, casting his fate, his life and death, in her terms.

If King's imaginary tour posits his presence before time, his sneezing anecdote invents his absence to draw attention to some of history's grand moments. In either case, it's clear that time is on his mind. And so is death—the death of time, the death of the movement, the death of hope. And to be sure, his own death. King comes to the close of his magnificent speech, improvised at the last moment in impossible conditions, with a nod to the threat of death, and his fears, as a way to eviscerate them. King tells how the plane he took to Memphis had to be guarded all night before taking off because he would be on board. He speaks as well of the dangers in Tennessee. "And then I got into Memphis. And some began to say the threats, or talk about the threats that were out, or what would happen to me from some of our sick white brothers."

King gives answer, but not before he zooms out from his gaze at time's start, by God's side, to the contingencies and accidents of history. The parallels between King and Jesus are apparent: Surrendering the perch of omniscience, he settles for the finite view of all mortals: "Well I don't know what will happen now." King's confession mixes resignation and defiance; the recognition of limits doesn't leave him helpless.

In the film footage of King's speech, his flashing eyes bore into his audience as he admits, "We've got some difficult days ahead." Because he couldn't control the future, except in his mind, he wouldn't worry over its outcome.

"But it really doesn't matter with me now." It's the third time he's said it in his speech, suggesting that maybe he really does mean it, but he has to remind himself that he does. The true reason for King's confidence is the only one he could ever bank on: that God had whisked him to a spot high above the misty plains of fear and doubt.

No sooner had King renounced the privilege of possessing a perspective before time, than he regained his bragging rights to beating time and all its buddies—fate, fear, and finality—by looking to the future. His automortological announcement is calm but insistent: "Because I've been to the mountaintop." King summons the metaphor of Moses to clinch the case of his prophetic pedigree. He also brings the Exodus story to a rousing conclusion. The camera captures King at side angle, his eyelids fluttering through his intense blinking, his head turning from left to right, his mouth wide open as his words tumble down his tongue with gravitas and grace.

"And I don't mind," King says before the applause subsides. "Like anybody, I'd like to live a long life," he yearns. "But long-ge-ve-ty has its place."

King stretches out the word like a shoehorn in a pair of loafers. It's almost as if he wants to make the word that means long life last as long as it can, a linguistic counterpoint to his rapidly shrinking life. Perhaps he flashed back on his monumental speech in Chicago, where he declared, "I have no martyr complex. I want to live as long as anybody in this building tonight, and sometimes I begin to doubt whether I'm gonna make it through. I must confess I'm tired." His voice is rising to its upper register of melodious resonance. King's speech was a clinic in the use of the vocal instrument to vibrate in swooping glissandos and poignant crescendos. King showed that there didn't have to be strife between *lexis* (style, such as metaphor) and *pisteis* (argumentation and proof) as there is in Aristotle's view of rhetoric. In the best black oratory, style is not juxtaposed to argument; in fact, style becomes a vehicle of substance. Paying attention to how you say what you say doesn't mean you have nothing to say.

"But I'm not concerned about that now," King trumpets. "I just want to do God's will. And He's allowed me to go up to the mountain." The preachers and audience smell King's climax and splice their elation into his speech. "Yes, sir!" "Oh yes!" "Go 'head!" "Yes, Doctor!" King's automortology merges with his theology, baptizing time in the sweet possibilities of divine destiny. Still, it is a hard assignment. King knows that Moses ascended the mountain and spied the blessed terrain his people would claim, but, punished by God, he failed to put clothes on his vision. It's a risky identification, one that pushes King toward his death, both imagined and real, as if by now the two could be separated.

"And I've looked over," King nearly sings as the preachers behind him shout out more affirming vernacular

42

phrases like "Talk to me!" "And I've s-e-e-e-e-n the Promised Land." King's implosive intensity forces his jaws to extend to their full range. His eyes are teary. His brow is furrowed. His energy is concentrated.

"I may not get there with you. But I want you to know tonight that we as people will *get* to the Promised Land." The congregation collapses in ecstatic verbal release at King's every word. His phrases are weighed and measured, yet manage to flow in admirable economy.

"And I'm happy tonight," King reassures his audience. Perhaps he senses they have caught wind of his premonition, or have misjudged the effect on him of the threats that circulated in the city. He boosts them as he boosts himself.

"I'm not worried about *anything!* I'm not fearing *any man!*" he promises his flock. "Mine eyes have seen the glory of the coming of the Lord." King begins the hymn he had quoted so often over the years. Just as he finishes a single line, King turns suddenly on his heels, as much out of emotional fullness as out of a sense of a dramatic ending. He nearly collapses into the waiting arms of Ralph Abernathy, as Jesse Jackson stands near to offer compliments and comfort.

Less than twenty-four hours later, Abernathy and Jackson shared King's final perch when he met his day on a desolate balcony at Lorraine Motel. A single bullet slammed him backward to the concrete floor, shattered his jaw, severed his spinal cord, rolled his eyes to the back of his head, and ushered him into the infinitely vast region of interpretation that he had already conjured in his mournful meditations on death.

# THREE

## FACING DEATH

HAD MARTIN LUTHER KING, JR., NOT BEEN preparing relentlessly for the likelihood of that bullet, his final speech would not have been fraught with such meaning. His unknowing final request, to musician Ben Branch standing in the courtyard with Jesse Jackson that chilly spring evening, was for him to play the hymn "Precious Lord, Take My Hand" at the rally that night, and to "play it real pretty." King was leaning over the railing at the time, and in another moment of blind prophecy, bending his back toward his assailant, proving his assertion of the night before that "a man can't ride your back unless it is bent." He was smiling as he stood there, about to turn to his room and fetch a coat for the ride.

With this seemingly small request to once again have God take his hand, King's flight through time the previous night suddenly seems less off the cuff or pulled out of the rainy night sky and more contemplative, as though King had given many hours of thought to those stops. His choices in light of his death seem far less praising of previous eras and more circumspect. You can hear in King's voice a disappointment with these great moments, almost a crestfallen tone that more hadn't been done sooner for the suffering of mankind. He starts with the Red Sea and the march of slaves out of Egypt and into a Promised Land, yes, but then he eavesdrops on the great Greek philosophers, a gaggle of old white men who put the right to own slaves into philosophical law. Without Aristotle's assertion that "from the hour of their birth, some are marked out for subjection, others for rule," centuries of justification would likely not exist. And the great Platonic rule regarding slaves, "let us have the best and most attached whom we can get," is hardly a moral edict forbidding the ownership of other humans. Surely a student of philosophy such as King would not overlook these not-so-small flaws of intellect.

He briefly pauses to visit the Roman Empire, infamous for its love of slave labor, without which much of the old world's infrastructure would not exist, saying, "I would see some developments around there." What kind of developments, if not ones to abolish slavery? Next stop, the Renaissance, with all that it "did for the cultural and aesthetic life of man." Is it possible that King is pushing irony here, as his voice is more dolorous than pleasant? Is

46

it possible that he could be referring to the emergence into the "light" of the core belief that one man's interests can and should supercede another's? Is it possible that King is actually referring to the onset of the African slave trades, which grew in lockstep with the greed of the Dutch and the French and the British as they opened their minds and opened new lands?

Surely, you would think, King chooses his namesake as a moment in time where virtue won out over the evil in man, but there is no mention of slavery in Luther's theses, nor in his wide writings, except to speak of man's slavery to sin, even though he lived in a time when slavery was commonplace throughout Europe and its colonies, and even as he was asserting man's need to be both free and a slave in order to be Christian. Another great man, Lincoln, is accused of "vacillating" before he could "finally come to the conclusion that he had to sign the Emancipation Proclamation." Hardly a ringing endorsement of the great emancipator's moral compass. And why did King next choose Roosevelt, who declared that "we have nothing to fear but fear itself" about the "problems of the bankruptcy of the nation"? Perhaps because even when Roosevelt had the opportunity to put an end to the grisliest decades of lynching with the stroke of his presidential pen he chose to walk away rather than risk losing the support of South-ern Democrats in his upcoming reelection. Only those who knew true fear itself, like King, could know just how deeply it was to be feared.

No, King chose the moment in time where he stood that night of April 3, 1968, because he knew in his very core that, as Sam Cooke hoped only three years earlier, change was finally about to come. (Cooke's 1965 single "A Change Is Gonna Come" was released posthumously. But before his murder—like King, he was shot in a small motel—he let close friend and soul crooner Bobby Womack hear the song, which includes the lyric "It's been too hard living, but I'm afraid to die." Womack said: "It sounds like death . . . it's just so eerie. It gives me the chills, Sam.") That change had been growing up right alongside of him. He knew that with the inevitability of his death would come the time worth living in—the time when all men and women would truly be seen and treated as equal in his beloved country. Now was the time when his true kingdom had come.

Regretfully, the end of King's life was not met with the kind of peace he had so cherished. Indeed, 110 American cities convulsed in rioting. Congress of Racial Equality (CORE) leader Floyd McKissick said that King "was the last prince of nonviolence. He was a symbol of nonviolence, the epitome of nonviolence. Nonviolence is a dead philosophy and it was not the black people that killed it." Stokely Carmichael agreed: "White America killed Dr. King. They had absolutely no reason to do so. He was the one man in our race who was trying to teach our people to have love, compassion and mercy for what white people had done . . . We have to retaliate for the death of our leaders. The execution of those deaths will not be in the courtrooms, they are going to be in the streets of the United States of America."

Beyond the anger and riots, black America was blanketed in grief and sorrow for its most beloved freedom fighter. A 1966 *Newsweek*-Harris survey of Negroes concluded: "Martin Luther King remains the preeminent leader." Neither Carmichael's nor McKissick's skepticism about nonviolence as an effective tool of black equality could blunt King's standing among his people. The huge admiration King garnered became even more hallowed in death. Black America mourned King's murder so deeply because it felt like *our* murder. King's death felt like the death of black progress, the death of black justice, the death of black hope, because its most passionate voice had been sniped into silence. King was in the eyes of many blacks the key to a righteous black future, one that threatened to slip away on the horns of a racial dilemma: whether to support more militant calls for racial justice, including black power and armed self-defense, or to side with King's insistence on a more aggressive version of nonviolence. That choice was still being put to the test when King died.

King's death also quenched for a while the black expectation that political struggle could bring a brighter future. The *Newsweek*-Harris survey argued that King "had become a symbol of progressive change in policies concerning race relations and poverty." His death dealt a severe blow to the belief of many blacks that such change could take place in organized politics. As one political scientist noted in 1969, King's assassination caused "an emotional disengagement from the realm of normal political behavior." Since King had been "a symbolic intermediary between individuals and the political system," his murder "had a much greater impact on Negroes than on whites, at least as far as changes in affective ties to the political system are concerned." However, there was no way to "ascertain the duration . . . of the grief and disaffection provoked by the murder."

Fortunately, the black mood changed; black mayors soon sprang up in Newark, New Jersey, and Gary, Indiana. As King's trusted lieutenant Andrew Young argued, by "1970, the sixties movement was disintegrating, and it was necessary that those of us who had worked in the movement now move into the political arena ourselves, applying our skills, contacts, and experiences to this previously forbidden area of activity." Young saw "political office as a way of sustaining what we had done and needed to do again rather than as a deviation from our history of collective struggle." In 1972, four years after King's murder created a seismic shift in racial sensibilities, Andrew Young won a seat, if not quite at the table of brotherhood, then at least in the halls of political power as the first black to go to Congress from Georgia since Reconstruction.

If black folk were grieved and disaffected—if they disbelieved in institutions in the society—King's murder "had little impact on whites." The most "common pattern of change for whites, increasing polarization of feelings" resulted from "a sensitization effect" that reinforced "pre-existing dispositions toward politics." Many whites felt the same about King after his murder as they did before he died. As a white woman in Memphis remarked, "Had he stayed home in Atlanta, he'd be alive today." Journalist David Halberstam, who'd written a thoughtful essay on King for *Harper's* magazine in August 1967, registered an obituary of sorts for the magazine a couple months after King's death while noting that he had attended, near the time of his first article, a suburban dinner party among nice affluent white folk. "One of the wives—station wagon, three children, forty-five-thousand-dollar house—leaned over and said, 'I wish you had spit in his face for me,'" Halberstam recalls. "It was a stunning moment; I wondered for a long time afterwards what King could possibly have done to her, in what conceivable way he could have threatened her, why this passionate hate." Tony setting or not, she was hardly alone.

There were some exceptions. In February and March of 1968, questionnaires were sent to nearly ten thousand members of college and university governing boards as part of a survey of college trustees. These nearly all-white college trustees formed "a very elite group of people, generally representing prestige occupational positions and substantially higher levels of formal education and income."

A month after they were mailed—and three quarters of the way through the response period—King was murdered. One of the questions asked the respondents about their perceived similarity to Martin Luther King, "and since the responses were still being received regularly, a unique opportunity to compare pre-and post-death attitudes was recognized." On the Thursday of King's death, nearly 3,500 questionnaires had been returned, and along with the questionnaires returned over the next three days, were marked as pre-assassination returns. The 1,100 questionnaires received after April 9 were marked post-assassination samples. Of the pre-assassination sample, 36% perceived their views as similar to King's, while the number spiked to 50% among post-assassination respondents, a 14% change. When asked if King's views were "very unlike mine," 30.48% of the pre-assassination sample agreed, while only 19.36% of the post-assassination respondents admitted a big difference in views.

The survey's authors suggest several reasons for the shift among the respondents: sensitivity to current events; the tendency to idealize the dead, with a corresponding reluctance to criticize them (especially since "it might be speculated that many of those who were most critical of King while he was alive might be expected to harbor guilt feelings, as though by their animosity they had pulled the trigger"); vast amounts of information about King in the media after his death "could have resulted in more awareness of the purposes of the man's life and a consequent realization of a greater similarity"; and violent black reaction to King's murder "brought home to white America in a constant barrage from the media the irascibility of the Negro population, the potential for anarchy, and the threat of a militant alternative" and made King appear "moderate, even to many conservatives." As one white woman in Atlanta said after King's death, "All we hope is some nice, religious Negro will quickly take his place."

Despite his popularity among black folk, King's reputation during his life enjoyed something of a rollercoaster ride in most quarters of white America. King was seen at first by many whites as a Yankee-educated preacher and troublemaker who used highfalutin' words to upset the segregated Southern social order. The FBI's second-in-command called him "the most dangerous and effective Negro leader in America." When liberal and international forces embraced him—he was named Man of the Year by *Time* in 1963, and granted the Nobel Peace Prize in the same year—King, like many black jazz musicians, finally received wide recognition at home just as he had abroad. When black militancy and black nationalism got back in vogue in the mid-sixties, King's luster seemed even more polished in white America. Faced with the prospect of leaders like Malcolm X and Stokely Carmichael, large segments of white America proclaimed King a godsend.

King increasingly butted heads with the soft, safe image manufactured for him. The more he protested poverty, denounced the Vietnam War, and lamented the unconscious racism of most whites, the more he lost favor and footing in white America. For the first time in a decade, King's name was left off the January 1967 Gallup poll list of the ten most admired Americans. Financial support for his organization nearly dried up. Mainstream newsmagazines turned on him for diving into foreign policy matters supposedly far beyond his depth. Universities withdrew lecture invitations. And no American publisher was eager to publish a book by the leader. King was at his nadir in white America. In truth, in many ways, King was socially and politically dead before he was killed. Martyrdom saved him from becoming a pariah to the white mainstream. And given the cycles and changing fortunes of black leadership, his death kept him from ultimately, almost inevitably, being dismissed as irrelevant to his own race.

But martyrdom also forced onto King's dead body the face of a toothless tiger. His threat has been domesticated, his danger sweetened. His depressions and wounds have been turned into waves and smiles. There is little suffering, only light and glory. King's more challenging rhetoric has gone unemployed, left homeless in front of the Lincoln Memorial, blanketed on freezing nights in dream metaphors, feasting on leftovers of hope-lite, drinking discarded cans of diet optimism. Whites have long since forgotten just how much heat and hate the thought of King could whip up. They have absolved themselves of blame for producing, or failing to fight, the murderous passions that finally tracked King down in Memphis. What his assassin couldn't see through his viewfinder is that his bullet would shoot King into legend; the force of his report only thrust King into an even larger and richer life than the one he lived. If one man held the gun, millions more propped him up and made it seem a good, even valiant idea. And millions of others failed to speak out bravely against the brutality and evil that finally hunted King down and killed him. In exchange for collective guilt, whites have given King lesser victories: a national birthday, iconic ubiquity, and endless encomiums. He has been idealized into uselessness for the poor he loved, immortalized into a niceness that dilutes the radical politics he endorsed. His justice agenda has been smothered by adulation.

But blacks have not been innocent in the posthumous manipulations of King's legacy. If whites have undercut King by praising him to death, blacks have hollowed his humanity through worship. The black reflex to protect King's reputation from unprincipled white attack is understandable. But the wish to worship him into perfection is misled; the desire to deify him is tragically misplaced. Many black folk believe that any criticism of King is treason to the race, a blemish to King's memory. But this is the retail version of King's true greatness. It dishonors the way King earned his stripes as black America's general: on the battlefield of social struggle in the bloody trenches of history. The scars of his humanity are what make his glorious achievements all the more remarkable. He did not descend as a god to become human; he labored as man to become a servant like his God. The urge to erase King's deficits is flawed; the nicks and bruises on King's image only enhance his appeal and humanity. By idolizing King, many blacks are unduly harsh on present leaders and the young who are said not to measure up to King's standards. But a reminder of King's missteps and mistakes might hearten those who struggle to remember that one need not be perfect to be useful.

Andrew Young reminds us that there is a liability to enshrining King in divinity:

> Martin has become a larger-than-life symbol, almost a deity, rather than the flesh-and-blood man I knew. There is a danger in this. We should not lose our sense of how the civil rights movement happened, because if we do, younger generations, along with ourselves, will lose a sense of how new opportunities were fought for, and won. In blurring, or ignoring, the context of the struggle, the veneration of Martin Luther King becomes devoid of depth and context, and the ability to use his model to renew the struggle for a just and equitable society is lost.

Whites want him clawless; blacks want him flawless. Both options are bad for using King's death as a means to inspire the kind of social change for which he died. What then are we to make of King's death?

It should be plain that King wasn't killed by a lone gunman. His downfall was eagerly sought, even mandated, in a culture of death that choked segments of white society that feared black equality. Tragic elements of that culture remain in today's hate groups. Recalcitrant, even anachronistic, racists refuse to die, or recede into the mists of history. True, many whites have learned to look beyond color to character. They waive the suspicion and skepticism of blacks learned at home or picked up in the culture. They recognize the humanity of each soul.

But whites must not reduce the problems of race to face and skin; they must also see them in structure and system. But it is harder to see things this way. It is far easier to believe that we've made all the progress we need to make on race. That only makes sense if we believe that personal behavior is the key to change—that whites should alter their actions to lessen, or destroy, racism, and that blacks in good faith should act as if such changes have occurred and take advantage of the opportunities at hand. To be sure, attitudes and beliefs among influential whites play a big role in distributing goods that matter to blacks: a job, a car, or a mortgage. But overcoming personal bigotry doesn't solve stubborn structural issues like chronic unemployment, racial profiling, educational inequity, radical poverty, gross over-imprisonment, and the enduring reluctance to hire black men. It takes more than enlightenment to solve these problems; goodwill alone can't heal these bleeding sores on the body politic. It takes the kind of sharp thinking about deep structures and faulty systems that King spoke of—and that may have, in part, caused his death. As Andrew Young argues, King survived challenging the "racial status quo," but was murdered when he "began to address poverty and war," and to "challenge in an even more fundamental way the basic structure of the American economy." He was murdered on the first-year anniversary of his bold public statement against the war in Vietnam. Given the government's rabid pursuit of the beleaguered minister, it's not hard to see how one might think this was more than mere coincidence or a lucky, opportunistic strike.

White Americans must also demand the truth about how elements of our government, especially the FBI under J. Edgar Hoover, tried to destroy King's career, marriage, and ultimately, his life. Hoover was obsessed with King, using illegal and immoral methods to tarnish his leadership by claiming he was a communist, by alleging financial malfeasance, snooping on King's sex life, and withholding information about death threats. King's financial integrity was above reproach; Hoover's attempts to paint him as a greedy minister were unsuccessful. Hoover's maniacal pursuit of King also failed to prove he was a communist, though his advisers Stanley Levison and Jack O'Dell had varying degrees of connection to the communist party and leftist organizations.

There was a valid history between communist organizations and the civil rights movement—as early as the 1930s white communist groups were the only people to come forward and pay for legal aid for Southern blacks accused of wrongdoing, most famously in the case of the Scottsboro boys. In the red scare that swept the nation, it was child's play for Hoover to link King's tolerance of progressive ideas to a communist-style treason, though it was Hoover himself who acted most like Soviet Russia with the unconstitutional tactics he employed trying to trap King. Hoover obsessed, jealously, over King's womanizing and sought to portray him to all who would listen as a pervert and moral menace. Despite ample evidence of King's surrender to fleshly enticements, Hoover sent doctored tapes of King allegedly having sex with another woman to King's wife in the hope of humiliating him and driving a wedge between him and Coretta. She refused to take the bait.

But it was the way that the FBI failed to warn King of legitimate death threats that is especially damning. Time and again, Hoover instructed his agents to leave King unwarned about, and unprotected from, death threats. In St. Petersburg, Florida, a letter detailing multiple assassination threats was sent to FBI headquarters. All the people named in the letter as targets of murder—including NAACP head Roy Wilkins, Atlanta mayor Ivan Allen, Bobby Kennedy, and President Johnson—were warned, except the principal target, Martin Luther King. Hoover said that King didn't deserve fair warning. Although King had sought federal protection in Selma, Hoover tampered with internal communications about the threats on King's life should he lead the march. Two credible threats loomed: one involving two gunmen from Detroit, the other a KKK killing squad from Louisiana. Hoover vetoed plans to warn King, scribbling "No" on one communiqué, and "not to tell King anything" on the other. It is beyond unconscionable for an official government agency to deny a private citizen information about potential threats, much less act to prevent the threats from being realized. These facts give a great deal of heat to the notion that there was a conspiracy within the government to take King down. It may also help explain the skepticism and suspicion that many blacks still harbor for the government, which many whites dismiss as mere paranoia. The fact of black paranoia should not undermine the legitimacy of black fear.

## STRANGE FRUIT

King's death must also be seen in light of a tradition of black death, from the first drowning on the first passage, the starvation, depredation, and complete annihilation of those who had any fight in them in the years of state-sanctioned slave-trading and owning, to the lynchings, shootings, stabbings, burnings, castrations, bombings, and assassinations that followed in the red wake of the

Civil war—a train of mortal meanings carrying a message of intimidation and fear to black folk. Lynching under Jim Crow was meant to prove the power of white supremacy. It was a highly visible way to keep Negroes in place by swinging black bodies into submission, hanging black bodies to hell, and burning black bodies into the black imagination and mainstream memory. The dead bodies of black folk were handed up as ample evidence that white folk were in control of every aspect of black life, and irrefutable proof that the issues of black life and death hung in the balance of white desire, permission, and power. As Billie Holliday memorably sang, black bodies were the "strange fruit" on Southern trees.

Whites who participated in lynching gained a great deal of joy and satisfaction from witnessing the final moments and subsequent death of black folk. Thus, lynching was a crime primarily suited to the optic nerve: a public spectacle to be viewed by the murdering whites, with cameras in hand, snapping shots of the offending black, often in alleged retaliation for reckless eyeballing, or the sexual desire of looking. Sex and death could be tied into one neat package and then strung up for the world to see. Sometimes, no other reason was necessary than the color of a man's skin. One lynching participant was asked why a black man had been murdered, and he replied, "Oh, because he was a nigger. And he was the best nigger in town. Why, he would even take off his hat to me."

"Negro barbecues" drew business leaders, elected officials, church members, women, children, and run-of-the-mill whites. Many of them sent postcards of the atrocities, a travelogue into the far country of Negro tragedy and the often literal black death of charred bodies. "This is the barbeque [sic] we had last night. My picture is to the left with a cross over it. Your son, Joe." Or, "This was made in the court yard in Center Texas he is a 16 year old black boy. He killed Earl's Grandma. She was Florence's mother. Give this to Bud. From Aunt Myrtle." Thus, intimacy and intimidation easily mixed; the most hallowed acts of family mingled with murder. Crowds of white folk posed for pictures near the mutilated black bodies. As Christine Harold and Kevin Michael DeLuca argue: "Lynching was an event, an occasion to see, to be seen, and to memorialize for others . . . Lynched black bodies were spectacles of white supremacy that helped forge white community. They were also messages of warning and terror for black communities." It was racial terror of black folk one body at a time.

In the early 1930s the death rate from vigilantism stemmed to a trickle, due in large part to the pioneering heroism of anti-lynching crusader Ida B. Wells-Barnett, and the interracial Association of Southern Women for the Prevention of Lynching. It was their specific outrage that men were still claiming that their hate crimes were perpetrated on behalf of women that fueled their cause. When in 1935 a homeless man named Rubin Stacy was jailed for begging door to door for food and consequently dragged from the jail and hanged, the movement finally had a case to bring to Washington. Anti-lynching legislation was drafted but withered without President Roosevelt's support. His feeling that he couldn't risk losing the White House and thereby end up doing less for civil rights in the long term is eerily echoed in King's last thoughts on the priest and Levite who pass by the naked, bleeding man on the road to Jericho: "And every now and then we begin to wonder whether maybe they were not going down to Jerusalem—or down to Jericho, rather to organize a 'Jericho Road Improvement Association.' That's a possibility. Maybe they felt that it was better to deal with the problem from the causal root, rather than to get bogged down with an individual effect."

After he secured his reelection, Roosevelt did what he could to attack the causal root by creating a civil rights branch of the Justice Department in 1939. Even so, no cases would prove out until 1946, and an untold number of lynchings occurred overseas during the war, including the hanging in Italy of Louis Till for the murder of one woman and the rape of two others in 1945. On the face of it, for those who favor the death penalty, this seems like a crime worthy of the punishment of hanging. But when you compound this information with the fact that seventy-five other black servicemen were hanged for similar crimes at or around the same time, it's much harder to find the truth of what may have happened so far away at a time of great crimes against God's dark people.

In a sad twist of fate, ten years later it would be Till's only son's shot, stabbed, strangled, and mutilated dead body that would wash up on the shores of the Tallahatchie River in Mississippi and ultimately enrage a black nation enough to come together and risk their own lives to get justice for their brothers and sisters. Emmitt Till was a fourteen-year-old Chicago boy who had been sent south by his mother to visit relatives during the summer. A disputed encounter with Carolyn Bryant, the twenty-one-year-old white wife of a shopkeeper from whom he bought a pack of bubble gum—some say he wolf-whistled at her, others claim he said "Bye baby" and "Gee you like a movie star," while others claim he propositioned her in a lewd manner, all on a dare to flirt with her from his new friends in Mississippi—led to a brutal, vicious, unspeakable crime, since the sin of a black male daring to flirt with a white woman was reason for murder. Till was kidnapped from his uncle's home in the middle of the night and savagely beaten to death before he was tossed into the river with a seventy-five-pound cotton gin spiked with barbed wire fixed to his neck.

Till's murder was so shocking because by the time his body was pulled from the killing waters, lynching, say Harold and DeLuca, "was no longer an acceptable public spectacle, though it was still an acceptable community practice." Racial violence "had gone more 'underground'" since "even the inexplicable disappearance of a black body made a perverse kind of sense. History had taught both blacks and whites how to fill in the blanks . . . Rumor and speculation now performed the rhetorical violence formerly exacted by the public lynching." Till's murder was meant to silence black folk; instead of being a symbol of white power and intimidation, as it was intended, it helped to ignite the civil rights movement by offering a visual reminder of the inhuman depths to which whites could sink (and sink blacks) in their desire to control black life. Till's mother fought the state of Mississippi to get her son's casket opened so she could see her son one last time. Once she had it opened, she had pictures of her son's disfigured visage printed in *Jet* magazine. It wasn't his sweet boyish smile beaming out from under a straw hat that galvanized the country; it was the hideous Munch *Scream*-like mask of complete annihilation that made the collective gorge rise and overflow. Freud said men speak to each other through women's bodies; it may be that whites speak to each other through black bodies. Till became more than a floating signifier of white power and death as they wanted. Instead, his bloated body and slack eyeless face became visual testimony in death to the power of black life to affirm protest and the need for spiritual response and black voice.

If lynching was forced underground in the politics of absence, in the nasty work of arranging the disappearance of black bodies, then the assassination of black leaders was an attempt to reclaim visibility in the ugly battle to use black death to intimidate black folk. Lynching was replaced by the symbolic gesture of collective death in the sniper's gun. When King was killed, it may have been a single man's bullet, but it was a tribe's desire driving the lethal projectile into King's neck. Lynching was aimed at everyday black folk for the most part; there was ghoulish democracy in lynching. Assassination is one better—it targets a "big nigger" and makes his death a cautionary tale. Medgar Evers's murder in 1963 is such an example. The message of Evers's assassination was clear: do what Evers did—integrate public facilities, schools, and restaurants, and organize voter registration drives— and you die. But the threat of death didn't deter Evers. "We both knew he was going to die," his widow Myrlie Evers said about her husband. "Medgar didn't want to be a martyr. But if he had to die to get us that far, he was willing to do it."

King's assassination was meant to say "We got the biggest Negro of all, the King of men, and if he can be got, then you're all vulnerable." There was a lesson to other blacks: don't try to do and be what he was, and be warned, those who speak up are in danger, are vulnerable. They will be terminated. If the best and brightest go down, then the rest of you must fall into place. Assassination possessed the evil potency of lynching—a former public spectacle pushed underground—with the advantage of leaving those who hadn't participated, but wanted to, both scot-free and able to enjoy a gleefully vicarious racist victory. The final irony in King's case was that what killed him actually made him and his cause stronger.

## LIFE GOES ON

If black death has been a staple of white terror, it has also become a physical, cultural, psychological, and sociological characteristic of black life. One of the challenges black folk face in the aftermath of King's death is to confront the cultures of death we have accepted and used. Black mortality has become, ironically enough, a style of existence. Death has become synonymous with black life in so many quarters of our culture, at times from natural causes—including preventable diseases that plague black bodies, like heart disease and diabetes. At other times it springs from acts of disconsolation committed against ourselves, like suicide, or from fits of rage, plans of conquest, episodes of envy, spikes of mortal passion, swirls of hate, all issuing from a violent vortex that draws down into murder. Black mortality has also become a norm of social exchange among those who haunt subcultures of crime. It is the way punishment (killing someone for offending honor or invading one's territory) and rewards (promoting a gang member for arbitrary or targeted death) operate in a culture of competition for criminal and illicit supremacy.

Black-on-black homicide is tragically real, though perhaps a misnomer: it's black under black, black over black, black against black. It's the politics of attrition measured in prepositions. King took up this issue when he responded to the death of Malcolm X, seeking to mollify black conflict in warring factions within the Nation of Islam while speaking against "dissent through murder." King said, "We must face the fact that there are some very ghastly and nightmarish aspects of violence taking place at this time and it does seem to be a feud between some of the Black Nationalist groups." King condemned the violence, and pleaded for its end. "I think it has to stop somewhere. It isn't good for the image of our nation. It isn't good for the Negro cause. It isn't good for anything that we hold dear in our country and democracy . . . I think we have to learn to disagree without being violently disagreeable and this whole philosophy of expressing dissent through murder must be vigorously condemned."

Of course, black mortality has also been made into a commodity in popular culture, in urban films—from *New Jack City* and *Boyz n the Hood* to *Paid in Full* and *Waist Deep*—and most notably in hip hop. Critics of hip hop claim that it is corporate-sponsored black death; they say that, at its worst, it is sonic genocide. The way hip-hop artists explore death both reflects and reinforces the vulnerability of black men—both at the hands of violent black males and in a culture that in the past has forced them to suffer in silence. Black elders fire on hip hop for profiting from an artistic culture of death.

Murder is even at the heart of hip hop's symbolic quest for capital: "dead presidents" is the term for cash, and there is, according to cultural critic James Peterson, an "abstract delight in the death of American political leaders. The complicated suggestion being: if living presidents won't represent me, dead ones will." Some critics of hip hop say it lends credence to the bloodshed on the streets of urban America. There is a lot not to like in the violent appetites that devour the creative imaginations of many entertainers. In such cases, the flattest and most tedious artistic expressions of violence and death hold sway.

But there are others who brilliantly, if disturbingly, wrestle with the problem of evil, especially the suffering they and their loved ones endure. Max Weber, the pioneering sociologist, spoke of theodicy as the effort of gifted people to make meaning of the suffering of the masses. The plight of the ghetto poor resounds clearly in the lyrics of those who survive to tell the tale of the lost and forgotten. Economic inequality, police brutality, and racism concern the best of these ghetto griots. To be sure, as with many talented artists, there's a great deal of moral ambiguity in their creations. They strike fear in many observers and make us uncomfortable, because they remind us how we humans are neither all good nor bad.

These artists maintain little distance from the evils they decry; at times, they embody in their characters the evil they'd like to defeat. It's an artistic ploy that is often overlooked or ignored.

Part of this has to do with the "keep it real" mantra that has been taken so seriously that its rhetorical pleasures are erased, and its signifying resonances removed, in the stark literalism of critics. Rappers are rarely viewed in the same vein of other artists who blur the lines between good and bad. Perhaps that has to do with the depressing social conditions these rappers come from. Hence they are straitjacketed into only delivering positive remedies for suffering, as opposed to adroitly, and dramatically, examining the give and take, the push and pull of good and evil in the human heart. Francis Ford Coppola can get away with it in the *Godfather*; Jay-Z is pounced on in *American Gangster*.

If King embraced automortology, the hip-hop artist who comes closest to his musings on finitude and the future is 2Pac, the genre's dean of death. As with many artists—notably Scarface, who was a forerunner of sorts—2Pac was obsessed with death: the death of fallen comrades, the death he witnessed, the death he wished on others, and above all, his own death. 2Pac's theodicy was full of sorrow and lamentation, his voice wailing and crying, at once defiant and mournful. 2Pac could go from "Life Goes On," a haunting, mellow paean to departed homeboys, to "Hit 'Em Up," a vicious battle song full of death aimed at archrival Notorious B.I.G. Like King, 2Pac died violently—though, as Chris Rock says, one was assassinated; the other was killed. Like King, 2Pac grew bigger than what his already crammed life could contain, or imagine. The uses made of 2Pac's body and memory make him unlike King in this sense: 2Pac has become, in death, a signifying, trickster figure in the black urban imagination. He has allegedly been spotted alive on islands by true believers.

2Pac has integrated the gallery of secular saints in white America—Elvis, James Dean, and Marilyn Monroe among them—who have survived their deaths to become mythological presences, a posthumous persona. He is the first black person to attain the comparable stature of these white figures. These figures have permanent futures because they have useful pasts that point to important moments in the culture, or suggest unique insight into a movement or people. They are kept alive because their survival fills a void, serves a need. In 2Pac's case, his survival expressed the moral ambitions of despised black youth. Many adults read his elevation as a morally bankrupt attempt at equivalency with King. Instead, it should be read as a critique of just how that generation has been left for dead by its elders.

Black folk must also come to grips with how we practice *soul murder*, a term coined by Scandinavian playwrights Henrik Ibsen and August Strindberg. Ibsen says that soul murder is the destruction of the love of life, the capacity for joy, in another human being. Daniel Paul Schreber, a nineteenth-century German jurist who went mad at forty-two (and was made famous by Freud in 1911 in one of his long case histories) defined his illness as soul murder, which rested on the notion "widespread in the folklore and poetry of all peoples that it is somehow possible to take possession of another person's soul." The term has since been applied to abused children and traumatized slaves. Black culture—by its deficits and defeats and by its defensive actions to protect its interests and assure its survival—has generated pockets of pathology where potential is suspected and snuffed. We murder ambition, slaughter pride. A tortured racial history feeds this learned behavior, sustained now as a self-perpetuating cultural practice. We are skeptical of black folk who don't meet our narrow views of blackness. We are taught to despise and be envious of others who rise and prosper.

All of this is different from the routine and healthy criticism in which all groups should engage. I am referring to the pernicious self-doubt, and other-doubt—really, it's race-doubt—that is the ontological residue of collective self-hate. It is a centuries-old reflex borne of pulverizing suspicion of the beauty, integrity, and dignity of blackness. We snuff our children's ambition through despising their intellectual independence and emotional freedom. We target our children with vicious corporal punishment to make them obedient to what we think the Bible says to do to our kids. We beat the hell out of our kids, and when we do, we often beat out their initiative and ambition too. In the name of King's movement against all forms of oppression, we must be released, and release each other, from such degrading, deadening, deathly practices. And in the public realm, we hardly do better. We don't buy black, shop black, or even love black, because we think and have been taught, and often still believe, that our blackness is just not good or beautiful enough. King spoke against the lethal tribal practice of self-imposed genocide in his last years.

Finally, one of the ugliest forms of black death is how the poor are subject to a symbolic social death. True, the application of this term to the poor does not square with the natal alienation of the slave to whom it was initially applied—and who was alienated "from all 'rights' or claims of birth" and "ceased to belong in his own right to any legitimate social order." They were cut off from the heritage of their ancestors, made genealogical isolates. The poor are, however, in effect socially dead persons. They suffer social alienation: They lack standing, status, and protection. They are mercilessly flogged in the press, demonized by fellow citizens, made a football by politicians, viciously criticized by public policy makers, and assaulted by scholars and intellectuals. The stigma the poor carry bans them from the presumption of political innocence, of being good citizens; they carry the weight of social pariah. They walk in the door with a capital "P" on their foreheads. The irony is that King spent his last few years rescuing the poor, helping them help themselves through political agency, and forging connections among the poor of different races and ethnicities. If we are to resurrect King's spirit and work for what he worked for, we must love and concentrate on the poor for whom Martin Luther King died. He also prophesied that black people would make it to the Promised Land. It has been forty years since his death, the same amount of time the children of Israel searched for their home. In the time since he died, are black people any closer to the Promised Land, or are we doomed to a racial wilderness?

No matter who killed him—a bigoted gunman, conspiring gangsters, or renegade government forces—Martin Luther King, Jr.'s life was an anxious and dramatic march to the grave. Of course, all humans are born to die. But King knew that in all likelihood he would go earlier and more violently than most. He exhausted himself uplifting his country and race, but hateful forces hounded him to his last breath. King's ultimate sacrifice made America a better country. His dream has been richly explored—and exploited. His birthday is celebrated as a national holiday. But his challenge to America has frozen beneath an avalanche of amnesia. King's date of death shivers in frosty abandonment. It is clearly easier to salute a hero than face a martyr. That is especially true when his death reminds us of our demons and our unachieved potential. Facing King may not be all bad. We may meet the man who already knew, and forgave, our wrongdoing. We may also see the leader who asks us to use his death to better our country. King used the unavoidable fact of death to argue for social change and measure our commitment to truth. There is a lot to be learned in how King feared and faced death, and fought it too. What we make of his death may determine what we make of his legacy and our future.

# PROMISED LAND,

## OR WILDERNESS?

# CHAPTER
# **FOUR**

## **REPORT CARD ON BLACK AMERICA**

PRESIDENT WILLIAM J. CLINTON, JR., stood behind the pulpit made famous by Martin Luther King, Jr., and asked his black Pentecostal audience a simple question: "If Martin Luther King . . . were to reappear by my side today, and give us a report card on the last twenty-five years, what would he say?" By 1993 much had changed—opportunity had blossomed but so had despondency. The black upper class soared, the middle class rose, then dipped, and the black lower class sunk so low that its children were killing each other over scraps of imagined nothingness. Never before had America seen such a chasm between rich and poor, a disparity that was amplified in the blight of inner-city blacks as they were forced to watch the explosive wealth of their upper-crust brethren fail to drop the crumbs of prosperity down from its banquet tables.

Some of the policies of the Clinton administration drove great change into the black economy, moving forward agendas like affirmative action and opening doors to black folk as high-placed officials in government. As Clinton stood before his audience, he believed the time had come to evoke King's message as a means to castigate black America for leaving behind the poorest among them, for not practicing what King had so urgently preached. Clinton dared in his homily to perform King's own act of *prosopopeia*—speaking as if you are someone else who is not present—by addressing the "great crisis of the spirit" that gripped black America by serving as both the slain prophet's historical secretary and philosophical ventriloquist.

Clinton confessed that he never dreamed he "would ever have a chance to come to this hallowed place where Martin Luther King gave his last sermon." The chance to be where King last spoke was thrilling; the temptation to *be* King speaking was irresistible. And though it would be five years before Toni Morrison famously dubbed Clinton "America's first black president," Clinton did not shy away from the already much-implied honorific nor the opportunities extended to him in this cherished role. But as proved in the bitter fallout over Clinton's controversial campaigning for his wife Hillary's 2008 bid for the Oval Office he once occupied—where he was accused of enflaming rather than dousing racial passions—it may be an honor the Southern politician took too far, and certainly too literally.

In his brief speech, Clinton worked from the same bag of rhetorical invention as King. While King imagined himself standing next to God, Clinton imagined himself standing next to King. Both men cloaked themselves in authority—one divine, the other as close to divine as an American black man has come—to take a trip through time to tell on the present. King stood outside of time before coming to rest in his own era. Clinton resurrected King to speak to the black world in the generation that has lapsed since his death. King largely reported his part of the conversation with God while speaking briefly in the Almighty's voice. Clinton, on the other hand, borrowed King's baritone extensively.

"'You did a good job,' he would say," Clinton mused. "'Voting and electing people who formerly were not electable because of the color of their skin.'" Clinton-as-King praises black political power and the freedom of blacks to live where they choose. He also praises black folk doing well in the military and the broadening of the black middle class. Then Clinton's King gets to the core of his assessment. "But he would say, 'I did not live and die to see the American family destroyed.'" And he didn't die so kids could gun each other down with automatic weapons and build fortunes on drug dealing and destroying lives. Clinton's version of King says he fought for freedom, but not the freedom to abandon children and families. Clinton's King says he "fought to stop white people from being so filled with hate that they would wreak violence on black people," but not "for the right of black people to murder other black people." Clinton then reasoned in his own voice that as government has to make changes "from the outside in" (including passing a crime bill, overhauling the health care system, and creating more jobs), black folk have to make changes "from the inside out . . . sometimes all the answers have to come from the values and the stirrings and the voices that speak to us from within."

In a clever use of empathy, Clinton used King's voice to castigate King's followers—and included himself by claiming the dead leader would be disappointed that "we would have abused our freedom this way," and went on to connect himself to the people in the room through his spiritual heart. From this unimpeachable position of solidarity, Clinton also argued that black crime, violence, family and community breakdown, drug and employment problems, and children impregnating each other without thought to the consequences had finally prompted the nation to address what Clinton later called "public pathology."

Switching back to King, he said the civil rights leader would praise our victory in the cold war, remark on the perks of technology, and acknowledge that hard work and playing by the rules can get you into a good college. But then Clinton passionately, poignantly asked, "How would we explain to him all these kids getting killed and killing each other? How would we justify the things that we permit that no other country in the world would permit? How could we explain that we gave people the freedom to succeed, and we created conditions in which millions abuse that freedom to destroy the things that make life worth living—and life itself?" Answering himself Clinton concluded somberly. "We cannot."

In a strange twist of fate, it was the policies put in place by another president, Franklin Delano Roosevelt, which first lifted many blacks out of poverty by creating programs that would today be labeled "workfare." And though these programs were not specifically designed with blacks in mind, it would be the poorest Americans who benefited most—and most of the poorest were black. The New Deal brought relief to the rural poor and funneled money into communities to create jobs, not handouts. Ironically, it would also be some of these same programs that would disenfranchise the already working poor, in particular sharecroppers, tenants, and farm laborers, none of whom were provided for in the Agricultural Adjustment Act of 1933. This particular piece of legislation would ultimately lay the groundwork for the kinds of farm subsidies that would eventually undermine the small family farm and drive even more poor rural blacks into urban environments in search of unskilled factory jobs. And it would be in the urban environment, where black parents were working numerous low-paying shifts to keep their small households afloat, that largely unchecked black youths would eventually turn to and on each other.

It was also Roosevelt's use of a coalition of "liberals" that would first unwittingly pair African Americans and communist organizations—long before communism became a cudgeling fear—in a way that would be used against both constituencies for the next fifty years. Though the policies of the New Deal helped at least half of black America, the other half would be forced into a deeper struggle—foremost due to the intensifying hatred of the supremacists around them as black men and women had increased opportunity to become "presentable" and "articulate," and more akin to white mainstream culture and possibility than they had ever dared to imagine. The New Deal showed them they could have a place at the table, even as that table was being burned along with their churches. By funneling some poor blacks into work and others into relief situations, Roosevelt's brilliant solution to the Depression created a definable schism within black culture whose repercussions are felt to this day.

Forty years after King's death, and fifteen years after Clinton's speech, the question of King's report card on black America deserves an answer. Whether black folk have set foot in the Promised Land, or got lost in the wilderness, depends on whom you ask and what you see. Quarters of black America have boomed into the upper reaches of prosperity. The wealthiest black folk, and the merely rich, have fared very well, more annoyed than trumped by racial beliefs and barriers. Due in large part to affirmative action, the upper-middle classes continue to rise, but their arc of triumph sometimes dead-ends in ceilings lowered on their professional ambitions, in particular for black women. The lower-middle and middle-middle classes are struggling but, to varying degrees, maintaining. The lower classes, meanwhile, are suffering greatly. The working poor are barely surviving, while the black impoverished—variously called the permanently poor, the ghetto poor, the underclass, or the "outer class" because they are banished to the outskirts of prosperity and respect—are struggling against the odds to eek out a living.

How are we to reconcile King's vision of a Promised Land for blacks with the stubborn reality of a wilderness for too many? On top of this, or perhaps roiling beneath it, a bitter civil war waged from the inside bloodies black America. Among the greatest casualties are typically the defenseless poor. They are further disgraced by the neglect, or indifference, of their more fortunate kin. Well-positioned critics in the ruling black class snipe at the poor at the same time as they offer amnesty to their mainstream enemies. When staunchly conservative social critics witness the black fortunate lambasting their poorer brothers and sisters, it offers insurance against the charge of racial insensitivity. After all, if well-heeled blacks are harshly judging them, how can whites who make similar comments be accused of indifference to the black poor? The bitter criticisms of the black elite also embolden radical conservatives to take similarly hard-line stances that oppose social and political help for the most vulnerable. And the poor are wounded by friendly fire; even the poor learn to loathe themselves and attack other poor people. Now more than ever we need King's wisdom and fire, and his love, for the most vulnerable and violated members of our community. These qualities must be kept in mind as we grapple toward the Promised Land and judge our progress through his eyes.

King would have agreed with portions of Clinton's speech, especially the need for more jobs and health care, but he would have surely quarreled with many of Clinton's contentions and positions. Praising the end of the cold war? Sure, but not so much because of what *they* were doing to us as what *we* were doing to ourselves. McCarthyism and the red scare allowed Congress and the FBI the pretense of making a historical connection between communist groups and African Americans a valid excuse to violate King's, and untold other Americans', civil liberties. Elevating people to the top of the military? King might have applauded Colin Powell's achievement, but he eventually spoke vehemently as a pacifist against wars hot and cold, and might not have been so happy with Powell's role in the Bush administration's march to war. King would have certainly opposed Clinton's subsequent welfare reform legislation, about which Clinton himself later admitted that most "advocates for the poor and for legal immigration, and several people in my cabinet . . . opposed . . . because it ended the federal guarantee of a fixed monthly benefit to welfare recipients, had a five-year limit on welfare benefits, cut overall spending on the food stamp program, and denied food stamps and medical care to low-income illegal immigrants." King advocated a guaranteed annual income for the poor and worked with welfare rights advocates to secure stronger, not weaker, benefits from the government.

Perhaps most troubling is how Clinton recruits King into the battle over ghetto violence and domestic disintegration among the poor. King had a profoundly different take on the issue than his self-appointed amanuensis—Clinton clearly didn't take good notes. While King opposed inner-city mayhem—in his time a lot of it had to do with riots—he traced the link between the ghetto and our government in denouncing violence. "As I have walked among the desperate, rejected and angry young men, I have told them that Molotov cocktails and rifles would not solve their problems," King said. "Their questions [about America using violence to solve its problems] hit home, and I knew that I could never again raise my voice against the violence of the oppressed in the ghettos without having first spoken clearly to the greatest purveyor of violence in the world today—my own government." And King would have never signed on to a Clinton crime bill that turned on segregated consumption: plainly stated, black offenders who smoked crack cocaine received much harsher sentences than white offenders who sniffed powder cocaine.

Though King had only a short lens to look through, he wasn't nearly as convinced as Clinton that the civil rights movement had done much for the black poor. King went so far as to say in 1966 that the Civil Rights Act of 1964 and the Voting Rights Act of 1965 had done little to better the plight of either Southern or Northern poor blacks. King charged that these "legislative and judicial victories did very little to improve" Northern ghettos or "penetrate the lower depths of Negro deprivation." King said "the changes that came about" because of civil rights struggle were "at best surface changes, they were not really substantive changes." The changes that came were "limited mainly to the Negro middle class." Because the condition of the black poor had worsened, King argued in February 1968 for "a redistribution of economic power."

That remedy is often written off by detractors as just another liberal ruse to mask what is considered the true source of the problem: the cultural pathologies and plagues of the poor. Clinton isn't alone in pinning the weight of cultural resurrection on blacks themselves. It has become fashionable among many critics to claim that the biggest harm to black America is self-imposed. Racism, it is claimed, has largely run its course, and now only the ambition and fortitude of black folk can save them; only their foolish reliance on old racial scripts can lead them astray. Blacks must bootstrap their way to prosperity like any other immigrant group that overcame obstacles to find its footing in the culture. What is lacking in this argument is that most blacks were not immigrants, they were slaves, and even after the core of the culture achieved freedom, they were set the kinds of obstacles—death, dismemberment, and denial of self—that no other immigrant group ever faced on these shores. Bearing that in mind, King still always encouraged personal responsibility, but he frowned on those who demanded poor black folk to do for themselves what the government automatically had done for businesses and white farmers after slavery.

"At the very same time that America refused to give the Negro any land," King said, "through an act of Congress our government was giving away millions of acres of land in the West and the Midwest, which meant it was willing to undergird its white peasants from Europe with an economic floor." King wailed indignantly at the nation's unjust demand for self-reliance from black folk while forgetting how white immigrants were offered education, agriculture, and subsidies. "But not only did they give them land, they built land grant colleges with government money to teach them how to farm. Not only that, they provided county agents to further their expertise in farming. Not only that, they provided low interest rates in order that they could mechanize their farms." It was not lost on King how white privilege and government support contrasted sharply to—and ultimately reinforced—black suffering.

King recognized that the call for black self-help made hypocrites of those who ignored the aid given the very groups to whom blacks are unfavorably compared. "Not only that, today many of these people are receiving millions of dollars in federal subsidies not to farm, and they are the very people telling the black man that he ought to lift himself by his own bootstraps." The call for blacks to turn inward and pull themselves up by their own striving, rather than wrestling with the massive structural problems of economic inequality that caused their blight, struck King as plain dishonest. "So often in America, we have socialism for the rich, and rugged, free enterprise capitalism for the poor," King said on another occasion. "Nobody has lifted himself by their own bootstraps." King also knew that there had been a time, and recently too, when the act of wearing boots, and thereby showing some small outward sign of equality to whites, was enough to get a black man hung.

When we examine the report card that King might have issued America, it may contain the rare A, but there will be more than likely plenty of failing grades as well.

## BY THE NUMBERS

Perhaps if we were to take a more realistic snapshot of black life—one that clarifies what progress has been made, and tells what lies ahead—it will help offset uninformed and exaggerated cries for black self-sufficiency. The big forces that have always pounced on black life—concentrated poverty, high rates of unemployment and imprisonment, persistent racial and economic inequality, family stress and strain, and violent crimes, especially homicide—remain largely undiminished. For instance, in 2004, the last year for which statistics are available, a black family of four earned a median income of $31,969—61% of the $52,423 median incomes for white households, and the lowest among minority groups. A quarter of black folk lived beneath the poverty line, which was roughly $21,000 for a family of four. Only 11% of whites were that poor. In 1968, 34.7% of blacks were poor while 10% of whites lived below the poverty line. And though 25% is clearly an improvement on 34.7%, it's still more than double that of white America.

Downward mobility is a fact of black life. In 1968, 45% of stable black middle-class children—those whose families pulled down $55,600 when adjusted for inflation—ended up among the lowest fifth of income earners once they had families of their own, a steep decline in salary that amounts to $23,100 in today's dollars. Conversely only 16% of whites suffered a similar fate. Even more shocking, almost half of black children whose families earned less than the median in 1968 sank all the way to the lowest income group when they came to maturity. Poverty begat greater poverty.

Forty years later, in *every* income group, black folk are statistically less likely than their white peers to match or surpass their parents' earnings, and more likely to slide further down the economic scale. Indeed, only 31% of black children born to middle-income parents now make more than their parents did, while 68% of white children have surpassed their parents' income. A common economic gauge of success in America is rate of home ownership, where we see blacks lagging far behind whites. In 1970, black home ownership was at 41.6%, while white home ownership was at 65.4%. Today, black home ownership has failed to reach 50% while white home ownership has jumped to a staggering 75.8%.

There is no doubt that education is fundamental to betterment, and when we look at the numbers there, the horizon is equally cloudy. In 1968, 54.9% of whites completed high school while only 30.1% of blacks matriculated. Things have improved dramatically for both races, with 80% of the nation's nearly 40 million blacks today earning a high school diploma. A very healthy number until you compare it to the 90.5% of whites—do the math and you find that at this rate not until 2176 will there be education parity in this country. And there are gender differences at work: black women routinely outstrip black men in education. Black males experience a precipitous decline in academic achievement beginning around the fourth grade, when they score 87% of what whites score on tests, and by the time they're in twelfth grade, those who have made it that far manage to score 75% of the white tally.

Once they get to college, 16% of black women and 13% of black men earn at least a bachelor's degree. Black women collect more than 63% of the college degrees earned by blacks; for every 100 women who earn a degree, there are 60 black men who achieve the same feat. In 1968, only 5.3% of black people between the ages of twenty-five and thirty had completed four or more years of college, while 15.6% of whites had done the same. The number for blacks now stands at 18.6%, still a 10% lag behind the 28.3% of whites with four or more years of higher education.

These forces hardly suggest stunted ambition as the culprit in black vulnerability and alienation. The gulf in black and white incomes is the monetary residue of inequality; it shows just how stubborn and systematic has been the denial of literal and symbolic capital to black kin. Greater education significantly boosts the odds of black folk getting bigger paychecks and more job security. For the working poor, that security all but vanishes into a haze of piecemeal jobs, part-time work, no benefits, sporadic rewards, and depressed wages—and hence, depressing prospects. The desire to work is large, the absence of sustaining work even larger. Black folk, like all Americans, must be challenged to get more education and at higher levels, but the courts must continue to demand better and equal early education so that every child learns how to love learning.

There is a pernicious trend toward subtle resegregation of schools across the nation as more and more public primary schools in urban areas are drained of upwardly mobile whites and affluent blacks who seek private education options. In rural communities in the South, it is well documented that at the start of desegregation whites who opposed mixing the races quickly organized and opened "private" schools that to this day tend to be almost 100% white-attended, just as the public schools are predominantly African American and poor. In Tunica, Mississippi, county seat to one of the poorest areas in the nation—a locale made up of a minority of white landowners and a majority of poor black descendents of sharecroppers—there stand two schools: Rosa Fort High School, which is 98% black and 97% "free lunch eligible," and the Tunica Institute of Learning, which is 99% white. When casino money flooded into the county from riverboat gambling on the county's shores, the area's coffers grew tenfold, but the public school money-per-child ratio remains over $1,000 behind the national average.

In May of 2007 the public school shut down for a few days when a man wearing black pants and a white and black T-shirt was seen wielding a rifle on campus. The man was not described by race, even though he was wearing a "T-shirt," which must have exposed some skin. Had this "man" been black, is it at all possible his race would not have been a factor? A "person of interest" was questioned and released, and the investigation was dropped after a few days. Imagine the same event happening across Tunica at the all-white school with a gunman who was presumed black. Would the investigation stop or, more likely, would it continue until someone was made to pay for the crime? In any case, the result of the incident was plain: black children were once again intimidated during a school day.

In like fashion, the courts must continue to protect an equal shot at universities and colleges through creative affirmative action policies. But neither education, nor retooling at the higher levels of work, is a guarantee that upper-management positions will open, or that ceilings carved from color or chromosomes can be crashed. The persistence of subtle discriminatory practices at work and school makes getting ahead a tedious task.

The dramatic downward mobility of black families, though depressing, is unavoidably metaphoric: sliding down a bleak spiral is far easier than rising on a positive trajectory. This state of affairs points to routine reversals of fortune met by the upward swing of white success in a culture where that success is both expected and supported. The ease of falling back and down for many black families screams the opposite: nonexistent wealth and social networks don't pass hands from one generation to the next. In 1983, the average white household had a net worth of

$287,900; for blacks it was a measly $54,200. By 2004, whites had a household net worth of $534,000 compared to $101,400 for blacks. To make matters worse, 29.4% of black households have zero or negative net worth, compared to 13% for whites.

Neither do the few resources that exist make it to the following generation. The subprime mortgage crisis will cost black folk between $71 billion and $122 billion, the greatest loss of black wealth in history. Only 17.2% of whites have high-cost loans; for blacks, the number is an astonishing 54.7%. The parental lift up the ladder of status is missing several rungs—gaps that accumulate as the arithmetic of negative calculation of all the goods and perks that go missing for black families, but which more well-positioned families take for granted. It is the tendency to see as natural what has been gained at someone else's expense—one's parents or grandparents, or other sources of both rightful and unjust inheritance—that often turns the beneficiaries of unearned privilege so harshly against the unfortunate.

Black folk may be far behind in education and economic security, but they can boast of a distinctly unwanted honor: Black mortality outstrips white mortality. The dramatic decline in mortality, and a big gain in life expectancy, a good measure of a population's overall well-being, has marked the twentieth century. In the United States, life expectancy jumped from 47.3 years in 1900 to more than 76 years in the late 1990s; 81 percent of Americans expect to live to be 65 years old. At the same time, there has been a significant spike in sex mortality differences: the female advantage in life expectancy hovers between five and eight years, up from two to three years in 1900. This means that American female life expectancy exceeded male life expectancy by 2.5 years in 1900 and 5.8 years by the late 1990s. Sex mortality differences are even more pronounced among blacks.

The same disparity holds true for race and socioeconomic status: black folk from lower economic groups are less likely to reach old age than members of other racial and ethnic groups, and from higher income brackets. Ironically, in 1968 the age expectancy for a black male was sixty years. After King's autopsy, the medical examiner reported that he was surprised to see the thirty-nine-year-old's heart had the wear and tear of a man who had seen sixty years—at that time an advanced age for a black man. The stress of carrying the hopes, dreams, and fears of a generation around for so long had ultimately worn King out even as he was murdered.

Black mortality increased a great deal between 1984 and 1989 while white mortality declined. Black males experienced a rise in death rates from HIV infection, homicide, and accidents; black females suffered from HIV infection, cancer at elevated ages, and diabetes. Despite a shrinking gap between the races, black mortality remains significantly higher than white mortality. Black male life expectancy still lags behind white male life expectancy by six years, while black female life expectancy trails white female life expectancy by more than five years. In descending order, black men die from heart disease, cancer, accidents, stroke, homicide, diabetes, HIV, chronic respiratory problems, kidney disease, and influenza and pneumonia. For black women, it is heart disease, cancer, stroke, diabetes, kidney disease, accidents, chronic lower respiratory diseases, septicemia, Alzheimer's disease, and influenza and pneumonia.

It is little wonder that black folk simply can't catch up in the race to live longer. Beyond all the shocks and wounds of living and dying that everyone faces, there is a grueling subculture of animosities, anxieties, and anguishes that end our lives earlier than might otherwise be the case. While the goods and privileges that black folk don't have cannot be passed along, the bruises and heartaches that are more than plentiful get transmitted like a virus. The weight of psychological hurt and existential brutality press down on the heart, kidneys, and lungs.

Unspoken, and therefore, unresolved racial conflicts invite bad eating habits and obesity, which are in turn enabled by a shrewdly specific marketing agenda. What could possibly be right about a Styrofoam bowl filled with bits of fried chicken, mashed potatoes, corn, and cheese, smothered in gravy and held out in black hands to black customers? At 740 delicious calories (half of those from the fat content of the meal) and 2350 milligrams of sodium—98 percent of the recommended daily allowance—is it any wonder that poor people, who can more easily afford this conveniently packaged and priced food than fresh meats and vegetables, are steadily becoming the most obese among us? We are perhaps the only country in the world where the rich get thinner and poor get fatter.

Self-doubt and self-hate bring self-destruction in bottles and cartons. Smoldering resentments and petty agitations lead to murderous fits of temper. Homicide is often the payoff for impoverished conditions; it is the unsubtle and undisciplined hatred of the other-who-is-like-me that blooms in the psyches of those who hate themselves and their plight even more. Brooding discontent with the racial ploys that deny mortgages and hike interest rates on loans leads to strokes and aneurysms. Recent subprime scandals have an unmistakable subtext: black life just shouldn't be housed in the same league and fashion as white life. Racial shorthand and racist Morse code can lead to debilitating fear and paranoia: did they mean to suggest I was that dumb, or were they just peddling the obnoxious pap to me that they'd give to a member of their own race? And the burden of trying to feed mouths, and a ravenous appetite for somebodyness, can eat one's soul into depression and suicide.

What all of these numbers offer is a portrait of black life that is hardly a reflection of the failure to strive for a better existence. Instead, the structural and institutional forces that beat down upon black life continue to hamper the flourishing of too many black folk and keep them from beginning to enter the Promised Land of social and racial equality that Martin Luther King imagined. This gulf between hope and the heartbreak that is the lot of millions of black poor is nowhere better glimpsed than in the social and economic circumstances that batter the black family.

# CHAPTER
# FIVE

# THE BLACK FAMILY AND BLACK INEQUALITY

THE STATE OF BLACK FAMILY LIFE IN AMERICA evokes grave concern, and graver criticism. There is no more certain and painful measure of the lag between Martin Luther King, Jr.'s dream of equality and the stark wilderness navigated by millions of blacks than in the numbers and plight of most poor black women, children, and men. From the suffering of children in families that struggle to gain sufficient economic support, to the difficult plight of single black women, to the unemployment and overincarceration of black males, the black family is buffeted by a host of brutal social facts that compromise its quality of survival and make a mockery of King's vision of a black Promised Land.

Nearly 70% of black children are born to single mothers, compared to 27% of white children, and 43% of Latinos. Black folk have lower marriage rates, and marital stability, than any ethnic group. Black families also have higher rates of single-headed families than all other groups. Thirty-three percent of black children live in two-parent families, compared to nearly 80% in 1960. Black homes have 45.4% single-female-headed families; white single-headed families register at 13.7%. More than 40% of black single-female-headed households live in poverty. In 1968, the number was not that much higher at 58.9%. Overall, nearly 40% of single-female-headed households live in poverty, while only 6% of two-parent families exist beneath the poverty level.

The majority of childbearing black women are unmarried, and the rate of out-of-wedlock childbirths is forever rising and falling. Unmarried women presently account for 69% of black births, compared to 22% for unmarried white women. There are 70 single black men for every 100 single black women, a figure that doesn't take into account the prison population or black males living in group homes—where folk who are unrelated live together, arrangements dictated by, for example, children with behavioral problems, troubled teens, or the victims of domestic violence. Contrary to popular perception, more black men than women have never been married. The percentage of black men who have never said "I do" is 43.3%, while 41.9% of black women have never had nuptials. By contrast, 27.4% of white males have never been married, compared to 20.7% of white females. Still, black women are the least likely members of society to marry: between 1970 and 2001, the United States marriage rate fell by 17%, but in black culture it plummeted by 34%.

Black children catch hell from birth. In 90% of metropolitan areas, black women experienced over a 9% share of low-birth-weight babies, much higher than the 5% target suggested by professional health goals. In 85% of metropolitan areas, white families with white children had a home ownership rate of 70%, compared to the 50% of black families who live in 96% of metropolitan areas. The typical black child in a metropolitan area lives in a neighborhood with a poverty rate of 21%; white children have a poverty rate of 8%. But there is segregation even in poverty: many more black children than white children live in *concentrated* poverty, where the majority of people who live around them are just as destitute. For instance, while only 25% of poor white children in Chicago lived in high-poverty neighborhoods, more than 90% of poor black children found themselves in the slums.

The same segregation plagues their schooling. As touched on above, there has been a profound resegregation of American schools. Here again, the numbers don't lie. More than 70% of black students in the nation attend schools that are composed largely of minority students. The segregation of black students is more than 25 points below 1969 levels, but there are still plenty of financially strapped schools that make a mockery of the judicial mandate for integrated education. White students typically attend schools where less than 20% of the student body comes from races other than their own. By comparison, black and brown students go to schools composed of 53–55% of their own race. In some cases, the numbers are substantially higher; more than a third of black and Latino students attend schools with a 90–100% minority population. In tandem with residential segregation, school resegregation amounts to little more than educational apartheid.

King hammered away at the belief—one that still resonates in the claims that black students are more anti-intellectual, and less interested in learning, than whites—that poor black children weren't as intelligent as their better off white peers. Although "one explanation of the poor educational results of Negro and other center-city children alleges that there is something basically wrong with the educational capacities of these children," King argued that our society hasn't given poor black youth "an equal opportunity at a decent education." He also drew attention to the wide disparities between urban and suburban schools and the unequal resources each received. "In 1962, suburbs spent $145 more per pupil than did the central cities," King said. "Even more disturbing is the sad fact that in 1957 the differences in educational expenditures between big city and suburb were very small; since then, the disparities have grown." King understood that economic inequality gave the children of the nation's elite a better chance to be educated.

The black family has been scrutinized, and attacked, since the domestic unit took shape under the pulverizing deformities of slavery. The black family was viewed by Daniel Moynihan, in a famously controversial 1965 report, as "a tangle of pathology" whose destruction by slavery flashed in female-headed households, absent fathers, and high illegitimacy. Martin Luther King was one of the few Negro leaders who refused to condemn Moynihan's report when it leaked out. (Of course King surely didn't agree with one of Moynihan's suggestions to overcome the ego-deflation of black matriarchy: sign up for the military to be sent to Vietnam under a program that lowered the military entrance requirements and funneled poor black men to combat. Moynihan said the military was the ideal patriarchy and "a world away from women, a world run by strong men and unquestioned authority.")

"The shattering blows on the Negro family have made it fragile, deprived and often psychopathic," King said in conjuring a depressing image to convey his beliefs about the domestic suffering of black folk. "Nothing is so much needed as a secure family life for a people to pull themselves out of poverty and backwardness." King quickly saw that the Moynihan report offered "dangers and opportunities." The opportunity the report provided was the chance to gain support and resources for the black family. The danger in the offing was that "problems will be attributed to innate Negro weakness and used to justify, neglect and rationalize oppression." It is clear in the public discussion of black families over the last forty years that the dangers won, drowning the report's opportunities in a sea of sociological and pop psychological assault that has enjoyed both political and scholarly support.

King didn't live to see Moynihan's thesis of black family pathology and an overbearing matriarchy challenged by scholars like Herbert Gutman, who argued a decade after the Moynihan report that the black family managed to remain close, strong, and intact from slavery to at least the Great Depression. Gutman's work drew from slave registers, Reconstruction marriage records, and subsequent census data to show that typical black families for most of our American experience have had two parents who remained married a long time. Before that, marital fidelity was prized and upheld in slave quarters; premarital sex was not encouraged, but tolerated, and illegitimacy brought no stigma. Of course, premarital sex and illegitimacy were staples of the white slave-owning sexual economy: slave masters pillaged and plundered young girls and women at will, and produced a constant stream of babies that would make the stereotypical pimped-out, family-fleeing, children-abandoning, absentee-fathering black male blush in embarrassment at his relatively low productivity.

Despite thwarted erotic exclusivity, black marriage bonds in slavery remained strong and long except when shattered by the sale of one spouse. Black fidelity was so vital that it outlasted periods of forced separation when one spouse escaped to freedom and left a mate behind. Family ties endured as some slaves stuck close even after escape, and risked recapture to see and touch their family's flesh again. Black families in slavery mostly rejected the white habit of wedding cousins. Instead, they embraced West African kinship ties, naming children after parents and grandparents.

Once they were freed, they even kept the names of former slave-owners to bolster family solidarity. That habit didn't just begin with single black mothers giving their babies the last names of the children's father. Even when blood relatives receded or were coerced into oblivion during slavery, black folk relied on strong patterns of fictive kin—a network of aunts, uncles, and cousins not bound by blood but brought into existence by the need to relate and love. That's why the obsessive demonizing of black families has obscured one of its strengths: multiple ways to gather kin that defy narrow views of what's healthy or respectful. As Gutman argued, Moynihan's report "was the last hurrah for the idea that there is one right way to organize family life."

There's little doubt that the black family is in big trouble. After the period taken up by Gutman's research, migration and urbanization repaid black families with

enormous grief and suffering. The black family adjusted
with great difficulty to the geography of deprivation,
reduction, and compression in the ghetto. Nor is there any
question that black families must shoulder some of the
weight and responsibility for improving our lot: increasing parental attention to our children's education; examining and discouraging some destructive birth trends among
vulnerable and desperate single young females; encourag-
ing greater responsibility for black fathers; and shifting
the dramatic emphasis on corporal punishment that leads
to psychological suffering and behavioral difficulties.
We must be honest about the black family's undeniable
wounds and scars, its flaws and failures, its illegitimacies
and abandonments, its dissipations and deconstructions,
its myriad self-destructions, all of which must be identified, fought, warred against, resisted, contested—and by
no means tolerated or excused—by black folk ourselves.

But if any entity bears primary responsibility for
destroying the black family, it isn't the black family.
Those of us seeking the salvation of black domesticity
must not dare overlook or deny the institutional forces
that dissolve kinship bonds—or separate sense from joy in
black families. We must be even more vigilant in pointing
to those who benefited from harming the black family by
raping, sundering, shattering, and brutalizing its members for crass financial gain. Those who say "That wasn't
me, but my foreparents" benefit by inheritance—by con-
suming monies and resources those black families should

have received but didn't, or by getting the cultural and psychological advantage of not being assumed to be pathological. It is even more grating to see unconscious beneficiaries of the black family's destruction flashing a self-flattering smirk of moral superiority, especially since their presumed ethical advantage rests on the immoral denial to those families of opportunity, legitimacy, and humane support.

The Clinton administration's welfare reform, with its institutional self-delusions—it didn't reform the system to the advantage of the most vulnerable, but to the convenience of its architects and perpetrators—doesn't begin to address the needs of the neediest. Black families can only prosper when we fix the problems that most hurt them—huge unemployment; racist and opportunistic lending and mortgage practices; diminished family and child care support for poor mothers; stunted retraining programs for black males who've been made obsolete by technological advance (while penalizing employers who practice discrimination in hiring black males); and the political erosion of early childhood learning programs that are critical to success later in life.

The plight of black males in particular has had grim consequences on black life. The 8.9% black unemployment rate is twice that of whites. For black men, the unemployment rate is even higher at 9.5%, compared to 4% for white men. In 2004, the percentage of black men 16 and over who were employed stood at 59.3%; for white men, it was 70.4%. This clearly has a huge impact on black income. The incomes of black men were higher in 1974 than they were in 2004. The median weekly income of black men 16 and over who worked full-time was 78% of white men's income. For black males between the ages of 15 and 34, homicide was the leading cause of death. Black men under the age of 25 are fifteen times more likely to die of homicide than their white peers. In 2005, black males accounted for 52%—or 6,800—of the nearly 13,000 homicide victims. In 2005, black males were even more vulnerable to violent crimes than black women.

If violent crime plagues black life, so does the lethal prison industry. Blacks are incarcerated at 4.8 times the rate of whites. In mid-2006, nearly 1 in every 123 blacks was incarcerated, compared to 1 in every 353 Latinos and 1 in every 588 whites. During the same time, an estimated 4.8% of black men were in prison or jail; the number for Latino men was 1.9%, and that of whites 0.7%. More than 11% of black men between the ages of 25 and 34 were incarcerated. Also, more black men—836,000—were in state or federal prisons or local jails than white men, 718,000 of whom were locked down, or Latino men, 426,000 of whom were behind bars. Black men made up more than 41% of the more than 2 million men held in custody; black men between the ages of 20 and 29 comprised 15.5% of all men sent away. Overall, black men were incarcerated at 6.5 times the rate of their white peers.

One of the legal loopholes for sending black offenders away continues to unjustly keep black prisoners behind bars: the abuse of crack cocaine. Under law, possessing five grams of crack cocaine (about five pea-sized "rocks") brings a mandatory *minimum* sentence of five years in prison. In sharp contrast, a first-time offender may simply possess any quantity of any other controlled substance and be punished by a *maximum* of one year in prison. The net result is that those who offend federal crack cocaine laws routinely receive substantially longer sentences than those who offend powder cocaine laws. The difference in the length of the sentences between the two has only increased since 1992. Typically, white offenders are the bulk of powder cocaine offenders while black offenders make up the majority of crack cocaine offenders, even as their percentages have declined since 1992, when it was 91.4%, to 84.7% in 2000, to today's 81.8%.

The big business of warehousing black and brown bodies in prison is more than despicable; it strains the bonds of morality and decency and threatens the civic compact of just treatment for all citizens. Relatively minor juvenile and narcotic offenses of law—ones that often escape notice when the subjects of prosecution are white youth—are magnified, and judicially marshaled, as the sick predicate for profitable confinement. Racial disproportion is wielded as a cudgel: the huge numbers of black men beat into prison can hardly be justified by the numbers or kinds of crime they commit. A lot of black men are simply thrown away for nonviolent drug offenses, as sadly nowhere are better criminals made than in prison.

There is a long and tragic history of black males being viewed as the scourge of Northern urban society. As whites fought to divide themselves from black inner-city life—a life made more nakedly brutal by white flight to safe suburban neighborhoods—they mischaracterized black males as the source of social decay. Black males were blamed for everything that made black life in the inner city harsh: crime, poverty, and drug addiction. There can be no denying in hindsight that the ballyhooed war on drugs of the 1980s was a war on black and brown men. President Reagan and members of his administration targeted young men of color as the source of urban suffering and sought to drag them to jail in the greatest wave of mass imprisonment in U.S. history. Ironically, the eighties were typified by the enormous use of powder cocaine in the halls of business and entertainment. Add to this the sudden appearance of crack in the inner cities at the same time that an illegal war was being waged in Nicaragua—a war that funneled the cheap narcotic straight into the hands of drug dealers as guns were ultimately exchanged for thousands of black men's souls. Finally poor blacks could afford a white man's escapist luxury on a mass scale. "Equality" had found its unconscionable level.

The life of poor black folk is caught between crime and punishment. Most critics argue that those of us who beg for rationality and clarity, and for consistency and fairness, in the criminal justice system are seeking amnesty for all black criminals or an escape of responsibility for misbehavior. Neither is true. Criminals should be held accountable for their crimes. The practice of murder to resolve conflicts has ravaged too many poor communities and must be opposed with every bit of our strength. We must preach against it, legislate against it, and march against it; but we must also demand an end to the economic and social ills that make murder a convenient tool to express aggression and secure goods in a perverted moral outlook—largely at the expense of other poor people.

Too often, however, segregation and racism penetrate even the depths of criminality: white offenders routinely get treated to a brand of justice that differs greatly from that meted out to black and other minorities. We need standards of criminal justice, and punishment for offense, that are, like Fox News is supposed to be, fair and balanced. A criminal justice system is criminal when it is ruined by racial preference and white privilege. The Jena Six case is but one instance of this infuriating and unjust divergence.

The Jena Six is a group of six black teenagers from Jena, Louisiana, who were charged in the December 2006 beating of Justin Barker, a white teenager at Jena High School. The beating came on the heels of several racially charged incidents in the town—including three white students who hung nooses from a tree at Jena High School—after a black student sought permission from a school administrator to sit under the school's "white tree," reserved exclusively by local custom for white students. The Jena Six case sparked protests that the arrests and subsequent charges were excessive and racially unjust. White Jena youth involved in other incidents were given far lighter penalties.

On September 20, 2007, thousands of protesters marched on Jena in one of the largest civil rights demonstrations in years. Mychal Bell, the only Jena Six member who has been tried—he was originally charged with attempted murder, though the charges were reduced with wide outcry—had his conviction of aggravated battery and conspiracy set aside because it was determined he should have been tried as a juvenile. Bell eventually pled guilty to a reduced charge of battery and agreed to testify against the other defendants should they face trial. Bell was sentenced to eighteen months, with credit for time he'd already served.

Unfortunately, the plight of the Jean Six is not unique. The overprosecution and overincarceration of black youth occurs with frightening regularity. It has been apparent for the longest time that black youth simply don't get a fair shake in the criminal justice system. The same offenses that get white youth a slap on the hand land black youth in juvenile detention, increasing the likelihood that they later end up in jail or prison. Nearly a decade before the Jena Six, black youth between the ages of 10 and 17 made up only 15% of their age group in the

United States population, yet accounted for more than 26% of juvenile arrests, 32% of delinquency referrals to juvenile court, 41% of juveniles detained in delinquency cases, 46% of juveniles in corrections institutions, and 52% of juveniles transferred to adult criminal court after judicial hearings. These statistics show that black youth are vulnerable to zealous prosecutors out to throw the book at them while proving to the broader society that they are tough on crime. Black youth are often the trophies of success for unprincipled tugs of war between the custodians of the criminal justice system over who should serve how much time for which crimes. It's no secret that our youth get the short end of that racially braided rope.

Even though Jena Six occurred in the Deep South, black youth in urban centers across the North and beyond face brutal miscarriages of justice. This happens in part because of the persistent stereotyping of black youth as crime-prone social misfits. It doesn't help that many hip-hop music videos carry the image of black youth committing crime or glorifying the gangsta lifestyle. But we can't scapegoat black popular culture as the source of the problem. We must acknowledge that the lyrics and lifestyles promoted in rap music track, even mimic—but didn't create—the image of black male youth as pathological and deviant. Only continued vigilance by black folk will assure that our children don't spend more time behind bars in unjust overprosecution. We must be more determined to vote, protest, resist, organize, and mobilize against the cruel miscarriage of justice that too often lies in wait for our youth. As the outpouring of black awareness and outrage around Jena Six proved, if we don't speak up and act up for our youth, few others will.

If our youth are targets of an unjust war, so are the poorest black Americans. The black poor have been made a political piñata: public policy makers, politicians, and cultural critics of varying stripes blindfold themselves to the dignity and humanity of the poor to strike at them with vicious stereotypes, and often hardened hearts, savoring from their broken images the sweet but soulless satisfaction of defeating the already defeated. In our day, this may even be truer of the black elite—whom I have elsewhere called the Afristocracy—than the white mainstream. Wealthy blacks, rich blacks, upper-middle-class blacks and solidly middle-class blacks have declared war on the poor. They have heaped burning coals of disdain and outright hatred on their heads.

It is not that the animosity isn't old; what is relatively new is the way it has gone public. Black elites have routinely and mercilessly hammered the poor behind the walls of black civil society and social organizations. After slavery, noblesse oblige prompted Afristocrats to uplift the race; but their aid and advice to the unwashed Negro masses often dripped in condescension and contempt. The moral refinement of the crude Negro has been a favorite theme of the Afristocracy ever since. The attempt to make poor blacks better has recently made rich blacks bitter.

116

Hurricane Katrina brought a remarkable downpour of charity to poor blacks from well-off blacks, but it was occasionally spiked with condemnations of the lifestyles and so-called lethargy of the least well-off. What role should fortunate blacks play in addressing the suffering of poor blacks? It is a question which, in a post-King era of black striving, too often goes unasked and unanswered.

# CHAPTER
# SIX

## WHAT WOULD MARTIN DO?

### Poverty, Prosperity, and
### the Performance of Blackness

MARTIN LUTHER KING JR. WAS A BLACK ELITE who renounced the privileges of fortunate birth to share the suffering of the poor. He was highly suspicious of charity as a long-term strategy for social change. King argued exactly a year before he died that "we are called to play the Good Samaritan on life's roadside," but that was "only an initial act." We must "come to see that the whole Jericho road must be transformed so that men and women will not be constantly beaten and robbed as they make their journeys on life's highway." King concluded that "true compassion is more than flinging a coin to a beggar;

it is not haphazard and superficial. It comes to see that an edifice which produces beggars needs restructuring."

King believed that charity was a poor substitute for justice. Charity is a hit-or-miss proposition; folk who tire of giving stop doing so when they think they've done enough. Justice seeks to take the distracting and fleeting emotions out of giving. Justice does not depend on feeling to do the right thing. It depends on right action and sound thinking about the most helpful route to the best and most virtuous outcome. King understood, and embodied, this noble distinction. People who give money to the poor deserve praise; people who give their lives to the poor deserve honor. King is among the few who should be honored.

While others make war on the poor, King made war on what made them poor. He moved in 1966 into a Chicago slum for several months to dramatize the plight of the poor, and to put flesh to the spirit of nonviolent resistance to "the violence of poverty." At the urging of activist Marian Wright Edelman, King began the Poor People's Campaign to bring national attention to the poor of all races. He joined with a coalition of activists across the racial and ethnic spectrum to fight poverty in a planned march on Washington, DC, in April of 1968. It was the first stage of a massive, aggressively nonviolent movement that called on poor people and their allies to take up residence in the nation's capital for months and, if necessary, shut down traffic. At the invitation of nonviolent apostle and activist James Lawson, King journeyed to Memphis to march and protest the mistreatment of poor sanitation workers on strike for better wages and just treatment. Before he was murdered, King planned to disobey a court injunction against marching to dramatize these poor black workers' plight.

King loved the poor and hated poverty. He never grew to despise them the way some black elites have. This was clear on April 4 when Ralph Abernathy and King ate lunch in the Lorraine Motel where he would be assassinated on the balcony in a few hours. The catfish special for the day thrilled King and Abernathy, but the waitress failed several times to get the order right.

"We'll have two orders, and two glasses of iced tea," King asked. Shortly, she returned. "You want one order of catfish or two?" she asked King. "Two orders," he said, holding up two fingers.

The two men passed their time talking about the court injunction against the planned march. They were quite hungry, and glanced occasionally at the kitchen door for the waitress to come with their order. When she finally arrived with a tray of food, they were excited. Despite King's clarification, she brought a single platter of fish and two glasses of iced tea. Abernathy was about to correct her when King stopped him.

"Oh, Ralph. Don't bother her anymore. She probably doesn't get paid minimum wage, and you know what the tips must be like here. We'll just eat from the same plate."

King was motivated by more than compassion for the poor; he brought ideas and analysis along in the fight against poverty. He believed that poverty was in part the weakened blood flow of resources into the arteries of deprived and vulnerable communities. Those arteries are clogged with failed political will and a severely diminished belief that poverty could be destroyed. King believed the problem could be solved—by guaranteeing the poor an annual income (progressive economist John Kenneth Galbraith said it could be done for $20 billion a year and even conservative economist Milton Friedman supported the idea through a form of negative income tax); by diverting resources from the war back into domestic social programs; by raising the minimum wage; by full employment (so that the Negro could be "freed from the smothering prison of poverty that stifles him generation after generation"); and by restructuring social and economic relations through "a revolution of values."

King argued that materialism, militarism, and racism were killer kin; these "triplets of tragedy," the offspring of greed and oppression's sordid marriage, were thicker than the political and cultural thieves who depended upon them to wreak havoc in the world. King said that when "machines and computers, profit motives and property rights are considered more important than people, the giant triplets of racism, materialism, and militarism are incapable of being conquered." He insisted that a nation that "will keep people in slavery for 244 years will 'thingify' them . . . exploit them, and poor people generally, economically." Economic exploitation meant that America "will have to have foreign investments and everything else, and will have to use its military might to protect them. All of these problems are tied together." He also argued that someone "has been profiting from the low wages of Negroes. Depressed living standards for Negroes are a structural part of the economy. Certain industries are based upon the supply of low-wage, underskilled and immobile non-white labor."

King viewed viable work as a key to combating the economic and psychic toll of poverty. Until black female activists challenged him late in his career, King framed his arguments in terms of the needs and vision of poor black men. "When you deprive a man of a job, you deprive him of his manhood, deprive him of the authority of fatherhood." King said this placed the black man "in a situation which controls his political life and denies his children an adequate education and health services while forcing his wife to live on welfare in a dilapidated dwelling and you have a systematic pattern of humiliation which is as immoral as slavery and a lot more crippling than southern segregation." King increasingly spoke of the "violence of poverty, which destroys the soul and bodies of people." Young black males became the "legion of the damned in our economic army. Damned to hold the dirtiest jobs, the lowest paying jobs—and damned to be not only the last hired but also the first fired when reversals come to our economy."

King brilliantly diagnosed the suffering the black poor endured in the struggle for freedom and self-worth, speaking of what he elegantly termed the black "discouraged." He also pointed to the hypocrisy of giving more analytical credibility to whites when they shared the same setback as blacks. King said black people "are living in a literal depression. Now the problem is when there is massive unemployment in the black community, the nation calls it a social problem. When there is massive unemployment in the white community, the nation calls it a depression." (Later in his speech, King said when money is "given out to provide certain rights for black people, they call it welfare. When it's given to white people, it's called subsidy.") King said that labor statistics show "that there is about 8.4 percent unemployment in the black community. But do you know, it doesn't include what we call the discouraged—the thousands and thousands of Negroes in this country who've given up, who've lost hope. They've had so many doors closed in their faces that they feel defeated, and they don't even go down to look for a job."

King was especially disappointed with the black middle class's refusal to toss in with the plight of the poor. He constantly reminded well-to-do blacks of their obligation to their less fortunate brothers and sisters. His words contrast sharply with the bitter assaults on the black poor out of the mouths of many of our present black elites.

> Now, some Negroes are more secure than others. None of us are secure enough, but some are more secure than others. And I'm trying to get it over to the Negro "partial-haves" to join hands with the Negro "have-nots." You know, we have too many Negroes who have somehow, through some education and a degree of economic security floated or kind of swam out of the back waters, the muddy waters, and they've kind of managed to get out into the fresh waters of the mainstream a little bit. And they've forgotten the stench of the back waters. Now I hope this will change. I hope that every Negro in this country will be in this movement for the poor, [and] know that all of God's children must have the basic necessities of life.

The black elite blame the black poor for their poverty, and hold them responsible for fixing the problem themselves. King said that if "society changes its concepts by placing the responsibility on its system, not on the individual, and guarantees secure employment or guaranteed income, dignity will come within the reach of all." King fought against reducing poverty to a matter of the personal responsibility of the poor. "We do much too little to assure decent, secure employment," King said. "And then we castigate the unemployed and underemployed for being misfits and ne'er-do-wells. We still assume that unemployment usually results from personal defects; our solutions therefore largely tend to be personal and individual." King argued that we "need to take quite a different view of the causes and cures of the economic misfortunes of the Negro and the poor and to aim at establishing income security."

King wasn't opposed to personal initiative and responsibility; he simply redefined it in political terms. It's most clear when he called black folk to account for the failure to exercise the franchise once they got the chance to vote. "And the tragedy is that even after we register in many instances, we don't even go out and vote. Now we must get up; we must rise up from our stools of do-nothingness and complacency and do something for ourselves. And in doing something for ourselves, we'll do something for the nation." But he consistently refused to offer a self-help prescription while ignoring the structural forces that punished poor people.

King took the black church to task for being possessed of a religion that talked more than it acted. He criticized religion for adding to, rather than challenging, social suffering. "I wish today, that Christians would stop talking so much about religion, and start doing something about it, and we would have a much better world," King said from his pulpit a week before his last birthday. "But the problem is that the church has sanctioned every evil in the

126

world. Whether it's racism, or whether it's the evils of monopoly-capitalism, or whether it's the evils of militarism. And this is why these things continue to exist in the world today." King tirelessly preached the biblical parable of Dives and Lazarus, recounting how Dives was rich on earth, while Lazarus was poor. King said that their roles were reversed in the afterlife: Dives was sent to hell, and Lazarus enjoyed a rich life in heaven. King said that Jesus never condemned wealth wholesale, so that it wasn't being rich that sent Dives to hell. Rather, it was because "he forgot about the poor."

Dives didn't go to hell because he was rich. Dives went to hell because he allowed Lazarus to become invisible. And Dives went to hell because he passed Lazarus by every day, but he never really saw him. Dives went to hell because he maximized the minimum and minimized the maximum. Dives went to hell because he allowed the means by which he lived to outdistance the ends for which he lived. Dives went to hell because he didn't use his wealth to bridge the gulf that separated him from Lazarus. That's why he went to hell. And if America doesn't use its wealth to bridge the gulf between the rich nations and the poor nations, between the poor and the rich in this nation, it too is going to hell. Now, I mean this. And I don't want the secure Negroes to end up going to a kind of spiritual, degenerate hell in their own lives.

King assailed black ministers for their material narcissism even as they neglected the needs of their parishioners. King told a group of black clergy in February of 1968 that they had to admit that some of them had "been lax." King said the black church had often been a "taillight rather than a headlight." He asked them to admit that "all too often some of us have stood in the midst of social injustice and yet we remained silent behind the safe security of stained glass windows." They also had to "honestly admit that in the midst of poverty of our own members, so often we've just looked around and ended up uttering pious irrelevancies and sanctimonious trivialities." King struck even harder as he encouraged his brethren to "admit that all too often we've been more concerned about the size of the wheel base on our automobiles, and the amount of money we get in our anniversaries, than we've been concerned about the problems of the people who made it possible for us to get these things."

One can only imagine how King would be appalled by the prosperity gospel movement in the black church, with its obsessive emphasis on getting rich and reading the bible through an exclusively entrepreneurial lens. The prophetic refrain of the black pulpit, as marginal as it has always been, is even more silenced in entrepreneurial evangelism. Prosperity gospel's most zealous proponents say that God wants all believers to drive big cars and live in big houses and make big money. Instead of criticizing excess, they rabidly embrace it; they slight altogether the structural forces that sustain poverty. Entrepreneurial evangelists personalize poverty; the poor either rise to riches or fall to being broke by their own sweat and prayers. It's self-help dispensed from a Mercedes-Benz or a private jet.

Prosperity preachers market their wares on television and mass appearances: an endless stream preaching in churches, auditoriums, and stadiums flow into audiotapes, DVDs, CDs, and books promoting wealth and well-being, all bought by their global congregation of consumers. Entrepreneurial evangelists are Booker T. Washington with prayer cloths and anointing oil: they spout a gospel of capitalism that endorses the status quo. King's dramatic attention to the poor is obscured, erased, or ignored. Entrepreneurial evangelists have perversely absorbed the prophetic demand for the gospel to renounce its other-worldly addictions and face the world at hand and turned it into a rationale for undisciplined materialism.

Although the socially conscious and politically active wing of the black church supplied King theological impetus for social change, it was always in the minority. That is even more the case now that the prosperity gospel has seized the black imagination at a time when the numbers of the black poor have increased, their plight made more difficult by a pronounced lack of either social empathy or critical resources. Now more than ever, the most fortunate members of the black community must helpfully address the plight of their beleaguered black brothers and sisters and find creative ways to bring the masses of black folk closer to the social and racial equality for which Martin Luther King hoped.

On the bright side, and beyond the prosperity gospel's grip of greed, there are those black Americans who have grabbed hold of their rung on the ladder of upward mobility in the years since King's death. Black households in the upper income bracket, those making $75,000 to $99,000, increased fourfold between 1967 and 2003, making up 7 percent of the population. And the numbers of the black middle class have significantly swollen. In 1960, there were only 385,586 black professionals, semi-professionals, business owners, managers, or officials, a number that ballooned to 1,317,080. By 1995, there were nearly seven million black folk employed in middle-class occupations, helped by blacks who became social workers, receptionists, insurance salespeople, and government bureaucrats.

## WE MIGHT JUST GET THERE WITHOUT HIM

Black progress toward the Promised Land King foresaw can't simply be measured in material terms. We must also understand how black intelligence and creativity have flourished, and have been acknowledged since King died—a measure of how blackness has been celebrated and supported, or at other times engaged or resisted, but rarely ignored. Black writers, athletes, singers, actors, and other creative figures have garnered prominence and exerted influence in America, a testament to King's vision being closer, in spirit at least, if not quite in the lives of the most vulnerable.

In his 1970 essay, writer Ralph Ellison eloquently addressed the question, "What America Would Be Like Without Blacks." Ellison said that American language would be the poorer without black inflections and nuances, since "whether it is admitted or not, much of the sound of that language is derived from the timbre of the African voice and the listening habits of the African ear." Ellison also wrote that without the presence of black "style, our jokes, tall tales, even our sports would be lacking in the sudden turns, shocks and swift changes of pace (all jazz-shaped) that serve to remind us that the world is ever unexplored." Ellison argued that it was our "tragic-comic attitude toward life" that explained our quality of black style known as "soul," which "announces the presence of a creative struggle against the realities of existence." Ellison contended that without black folk "our political history would have been otherwise"—no slave economy, Civil War, Reconstruction, KKK, or Jim Crow—and we would not know that the "most obvious test and clue" to the self-perfection of the democratic process "is the inclusion, *not* assimilation, of the black man." This led Ellison to conclude that "whatever else the true American is, he is also somehow black." A mere two years after King's death, the political urgency of Ellison's remarks, whether intended or not, could hardly be denied.

Over the last forty years, many black artists, intellectuals, and activists have transformed our society through their love affair with the sort of excellence King often encouraged. Without their contributions, America would not look the same, sound the same, or even struggle in the same way to bring us closer to King's imagined Promised Land. Writers like Maya Angelou, Toni Morrison, Sonia Sanchez, Edward P. Jones, Nikki Giovanni, Alice Walker, John Edgar Wideman, and Walter Moseley—like James Baldwin, Ralph Ellison, Richard Wright, and Gwendolyn Brooks before them—have reshaped American literature with their protean gifts. Richard Pryor's unruly comic genius spliced rage into social commentary and brought America face-to-face with its darker brother, opening the door for Eddie Murphy, the Wayans Brothers, and Whoopi Goldberg. Alvin Ailey's dance troupe—especially in the sweep of Judith Jamison's limbs—won appreciation for the grace of black movement, even as the rhythms of black tap created a heartbeat through the soles of Sammy Davis Jr., Gregory Hines, and Savion Glover. Jessye Norman and Kathleen Battle—as Marian Anderson and Leontyne Price had done—spiced opera with the pathos and charm of the black voice. Muhammad Ali's fists and mouth—both in the boxing ring and in the public arena—hammered home black courage. Like Jackie Robinson before him, who broke the color barrier in baseball and integrated American sports, and Michael Jordan after him, whose will to fly raised the bar on athletic style and standards, Ali's physical skill symbolized black humanity.

Black artists have profoundly changed what and how America sees—in the images that flare on the canvass as well as those that flicker on the large and small screens. During King's era, Gordon Parks peeked through photographic and, later, cinematic lenses to record the travail and triumph of black life. Black artists used Abstract Expressionism and social protest—and brushes, pens, invented materials, and found objects—to fashion the textures and colors of a new black humanity that challenged racial stereotypes. Our humanity shines in Elizabeth Catlett's *Sharecropper*, a portrait of a black woman that conjures strength and elicits sympathy created the year King died. It is glimpsed as well in Bettye Saar's *The Liberation of Aunt Jemima*, a feisty revision of the black mammy myth, and in Kara Walker's black-cut paper silhouettes, including *Insurrection! (Our Tools Were Rudimentary, Yet We Pressed On)*, which play with racial stereotypes to undercut them. And Jean-Michel Basquiat's powerful and disturbing art undercut the notion of a single, or simple, black esthetic.

Black artists also took to stage and screen to portray the contradictory forces that define black existence, and America's too. George C. Wolfe challenged narrow views of black life with stereotype-shattering and politically incorrect views of blackness, while August Wilson brilliantly explored the terrain of twentieth-century black life in a series of plays whose sheer elegance is a testimony to the black will to survive the worst that life offers. Harry Belafonte, a brilliant calypso singer who brought island rhythms to American soil, was one of King's closest friends, advisers, and fundraisers. Sidney Poitier was also King's friend. His elegant body of work—his turn as Virgil Tibbs in *The Heat of the Night* still resonates with a splendid mix of fury and dignity—combated the negative black image in Hollywood. Since King's death, the work of Spike Lee a generation later—especially his provocative morality tale *Do The Right Thing* and his magnum opus, *Malcolm X*, the greatest black biopic ever made—opened up black film. It cleared the way for John Singleton's poignant urban drama *Boyz N the Hood*, which enflamed the American psyche with the suffering of young black males, and Kasi Lemons's sublime ebony Greek drama *Eve's Bayou*, which added shades of complexity to black identity.

Without Poitier, and the talented and troubled Dorothy Dandridge, there would be no Denzel Washington or Halle Berry. Their sensuality and grace—and their irreverence as well—singe the silver screen. On the small screen, Bill Cosby almost single-handedly changed how blacks are seen. His cerebral Alexander Scott character on *I Spy* shattered television's race barrier in the sixties and was neither a lackey nor a buffoon. Cosby's Chet Kincaid character—a coach and school teacher who brought humor to his effort to enlighten his students—and his gentle patriarch on *The Cosby Show,* twenty years after *I Spy,* revived the sit-com and made him America's Dad, a title that would have been unthinkable a generation earlier. And Oprah's first-name familiarity suggests how she used the medium to build an unprecedented media empire that has given her a bigger and longer presence in white homes than any black figure ever.

The sound of America is sweeter, more soulful, and more sorrowful because of black artists. The blues drew from West African rhythms, work songs, chants, and spirituals. In the mid-forties, the country blues migrated north when Muddy Waters boarded a train from Clarksdale, Mississippi, to Chicago, making it the center of urban blues. The music's irony and tragicomedy, and its humor, too, flood the plaintive cries of Howlin' Wolf, the weeping guitar of B. B. King, the salty wails of Koko Taylor, and the artful hawks of the otherwise smooth Bobby Blue Bland—who lifted his signature warble from Rev. C. L. Franklin, one of the great innovators of sacred sound. Their craft testifies to how blues artists ministered to Negroes seeking consolation for the griefs of ghetto existence. More recently, Robert Cray, Keb Mo, and Deborah Coleman have enriched the art form.

Jazz, too, shifted radically in its sound during King's era, and afterward. While big band swing music had dominated the idiom, bebop emerged in the mid-forties as Charlie Parker—and after him Dizzy Gillespie, Thelonious Monk, Charlie Christian, Bud Powell, Don Byas,

and Ben Webster——experimented with chord progres-
sions, faster tempos, higher notes, and more dissonant
tones. With bebop, jazz went from dance music to an art
form to be listened to. Armstrong and Ellington remained
the music's greatest performer and composer, respectively;
and Ella Fitzgerald and Sarah Vaughn brilliantly explored
the American songbook after Billie Holliday's death.
Miles and Coltrane rode together from bebop and hardbop
to modal jazz. Later, Davis jumpstarted fusion, while
Coltrane pioneered free jazz. Each influenced American
musical experimentation while revolutionizing the sound
and shape of jazz. The present neotraditional movement
incorporating swing, bop, and ragtime blows through the
virtuosic trumpet of Wynton Marsalis, the first jazz musician to snag a Pulitzer Prize and head of the influential
Jazz at Lincoln Center. And Terrance Blanchard's *A Tale of
God's Will (A Requiem for Katrina)* is a searing and at times
mournful musical evocation of the indomitable black
spirit that has kept black folk afloat from slave ships to
Hurricane Katrina. Without jazz, American democracy
can't swing, can't imagine its improvised destiny.

Rock and roll was born as the modern civil rights
movement took off. Although they hardly get their due,
black rock and roll artists helped establish the idea of
black humanity in a large white fan base. Without Chuck
Berry's 1955 "Maybeline" and Little Richard's "Tutti
Frutti" the same year, all that came after them, including
Elvis, makes no sense. Motown was born in 1959 and,

more than ever, black sound captivated the white ear. Motown was home to two of pop music's towering prophets—Marvin Gaye and Stevie Wonder—whose politics and pleas for change were rooted in love.

The two greatest voices, arguably, in all of popular music—Sam Cooke and Aretha Franklin—both emerged during the civil rights movement from their base in the church. Gospel music—from close King friend Mahalia Jackson's trembling, triumphant shout to, more recently, Yolanda Adams's soulful, secular saintliness and Kirk Franklin's gospel funk—has lifted the spirit of black people. Gospel also willed its edifying groans and melodic sweep to golden-voiced R&B giants Curtis Mayfield and Donny Hathaway. Cooke twirled the country's need for love on the rollicking riffs of his haunting tenor, while Aretha's soul-shattering sanctified moans captured our yearning for faith. And a string of delightful divas has blessed the musical landscape; their fame and contributions are so integral to black life and American culture that their first names need only be cited: Diana, Dionne, Whitney, Janet, Mary J., and Beyonce. James Brown fathered funk; Sly Stone raised it. Ray Charles's mastery of it all made America see beyond its blinding bigotry. Hip-hop, of course, is the greatest development in pop culture in the last quarter century. If not for the furious poetry and elastic rhythms of rap's greatest artists—including 2Pac, Notorious B.I.G., Nas, Chuck D, KRS-One, Common, MC Lyte, and Jay-Z—and the soulful yearnings of the best girl groups—En Vouge, TLC, Destiny's Child, like the Supremes before them—black youth might be unheard and invisible.

Less than a decade after King's death, a monumental event occurred that changed the face of American culture and how black folk are viewed: the publication of Alex Haley's *Roots* and the groundbreaking television series made from the book—the highest rated in the history of the small screen at the time. From the very beginning, *Roots* counted as much more than a mere book. It tapped deeply into the black American hunger for an African ancestral home that had been savaged by centuries of slavery and racial dislocation. More than the sum of its historical and literary parts—some of which have been rigorously criticized and debunked—Haley's quest for his roots changed the way black folk thought about themselves and how white America viewed them. No longer were we genealogical nomads with little hope of learning the names and identities of the people from whose loins and culture we sprang.

Haley wrote black folk into the book of American heritage and gave us the confidence to believe that we could find our forebears even as he shared his own. Kunta and Kizzy—and Chicken George too—became members of our black American family. That's why no flaw or shortcoming in Haley's tome could dim the brilliant light he shed on the black soul. Haley's monumental achievement helped convince the nation that the black story is the

American story. He also made it clear that black humanity is a shining beacon that miraculously endured slavery's brutal horrors.

I was a seventeen-year-old boarding school student when Haley's comet of a book hit the nation's racial landscape. It immediately changed the course of our conversations around school and provided a powerful lens onto a period of history that few of us really understood. Until Haley's book, there was little public grappling with the drama of American slavery. Of course, the epochal television series that grew from Haley's text seized us in its thrilling exploration of chattel slavery's vast and vicious evolution. The book and television series also sparked the phenomenon of black self-discovery.

For too long, slavery had been an American terror that left the lives of black folk scarred by memories of pain and humiliation. Haley's book brought black folk out of the shadows of shame and ignorance. It also spurred many of us for the first time to speak openly and honestly about the lingering effects of centuries-old oppression. If the black freedom struggle of the sixties had liberated our bodies from the haunting imperatives of white supremacy, Haley's book helped free our minds and spirits from that same force.

*Roots* also prodded white America to reject the racial amnesia that fed its moral immaturity and its racial irresponsibility. As long as there was no book or image that captured slavery's disfiguring reach, the nation could conduct its business as if all racial problems had been solved when it finally bestowed civil rights on its black citizens. But Haley helped us to resist that seductive lie with a tonic splash of colorful truth: that the nation had yet to successfully negotiate its perilous ties to an institution that built white prosperity while crushing black opportunity. *Roots* was a soulful reminder that unless we grappled with the past, we would be forever saddled by its deadening liabilities. Since it was published during the nation's blithely romantic celebration of its bicentennial, Haley's book provided a touchstone for alternative history. Haley's book helped conscientious citizens to challenge the self-image of America as an unqualified champion of democracy and freedom.

The true impact of Haley's book is that it started a conversation about black roots that continues to this day. DNA tests to determine black ancestry are more popular than ever. Scientific advance is part of the explanation, but the cultural impetus for such an agenda of racial discovery lies with Haley's inspiring book. It is also fitting that *Roots* appeared the same year that Black History Week was officially extended to Black History Month. Haley's crowning achievement came along at just the right time to prompt the investigation of black folks' noble and complex contributions to national culture. Haley's *Roots* sparked curiosity among ordinary citizens by making the intricate relations among race, politics, and culture eminently accessible. Long before demands for history from the bottom up became a rallying cry of progressive historians, Haley's book practiced what it preached. And if he made missteps along the way, he nevertheless put millions of us on the right path to racial and historical knowledge that shaped our reckoning with the color line. Coming as it did on the heels of King's death and the rise of black pride and black power, Haley's book marked a significant transition in the public definition of black culture, and thus arguably forged a critical link in the chain of black struggle toward the Promised Land.

Black art and cultural preoccupations—jazz and boxing, baseball and blues, detective novels and black bildungsroman, opera and country, acting on television and the silver screen—have provided examples of black intelligence and humanity that, over the last forty years, have brought black folk into the homes, minds, and imaginations of white America. The civil rights revolution benefited from such black genius, and made a way for more of it to reach the American mainstream and even more of black masses. Black art's development is a sure index of the intellectual and artistic progress black America has made since King's death. But, of course, a great deal remains to be done to make black people truly free.

King's prophetic shadow extends across the nation, and black America, in the forty years since his death. We measure our progress in terms of his dream, but especially his heroic deeds on behalf of the dispossessed and poor. His example calls to us from his grave to resurrect the spirit of resistance to oppression and to fight for the lives of the most vulnerable. It also causes us to reflect on the leaders who have emerged since he left us too soon in the promising flowering of a new, more radical, even dangerous, path to social revolution.

# PART THREE

# JOSHUA

## CHARISMATIC
## BLACK LEADERSHIP IN A
## PROPHET'S SHADOW

# CHAPTER
# **SEVEN**

# **A MESSIAH MEASURES LEADERSHIP**

BEFORE HIS BODY WAS EVEN LAID TO REST, Martin Luther King, Jr., had slipped into the long night of myth. He quickly became the most overworked martyr since Abraham Lincoln. The folk who loved him got up the courage to say so; those who despised him couldn't afford to say so as loudly—their hatred of King was no longer in vogue. He'd gone from nuisance to saint in a matter of days. It took fifteen years to get him a national holiday, but as honors like that go, it was a heartbeat. George Washington received the same honor a long eighty years after his death. It now seems inevitable that King's memory would be forced to carry the burden of our deepest desires as a country. After all, given the racial chasm his death revealed, King—or rather the eminently useful godlike image of the leader postmortem—was commissioned to achieve in death what he had been denied in life: the forging of racial harmony amidst the conflict of color. The price paid for becoming an outsized American hero was the manufactured appearance that the nation had agreed with him all along. The last thing the country needed was the image of King being killed because he was more faithful to core American ideals than the white mainstream that bitterly opposed him.

A large part of King's posthumous makeover focused on his role as the consummate and, judging by the articles and books that poured out after his death, the *only* leader worth mentioning in the civil rights movement. Crowning King as his people's Moses began immediately with his organization's attempt to situate him in a field of rivals as the leader best suited to get racial equality for black folk. King was an intriguing mixture of inspirations and impulses: he was at once the most humble big black leader around and yet extremely conscious of his messianic function in the drama of black freedom. Paraphrasing theologian Reinhold Niebuhr, King claimed that "the battering rams of historical necessity" had thrust him into destiny. His calling came from on high.

As early as 1957, King declared himself a Moses to his people. "If I had to die tomorrow morning I would die happy because I've been to the mountaintop and I've seen the Promised Land and it's going to be here in Montgomery" was a refrain he would voice many times. He was constantly lauded as a messiah by jubilant well-wishers whose praise countered the vicious criticism King regularly received. In 1956, a Baptist minister wrote to King that "I have longed for a Baptist Messiah like you since 1932!!" And as King made his way to a mass meeting the evening he was convicted of conspiracy for leading the bus boycott, a preacher exclaimed: "He who was nailed to the cross for us this afternoon approaches."

As King's fame grew, so did the jealousy and criticism of his peers. Many older civil rights leaders resented how handily he rose to the top once he found his stride a few years after the bus boycott in Montgomery. Younger activists in the movement, especially those in the Student Nonviolent Coordinating Committee (SNCC), criticized King's hierarchical, top-down leadership. Behind his back, they ridiculed him for his alleged messianic posturing by calling King "De Lawd." SNCC's leaders, inspired by activist Ella Baker, promoted a leaderless grassroots movement of the masses. Later, however, SNCC leader John Lewis confessed that his group's version had its own faults that led to its downfall. "Anarchy and chaos," Lewis writes, "freedom and openness. It's amazing how . . . principles that are treasured at one moment as positive and healthy can, with time and a shift in circumstances, become forces of destruction." Lewis says that by the fall of 1964, SNCC had succumbed to such forces, and that "the precepts that had been so fundamental to us when we began—decentralization, minimal structure, a distrust of leadership—were now beginning to tear us apart."

There has been a big debate among scholars of the civil rights movement about whether it is Great Men—and the inherent patriarchy of the term has been increasingly criticized as the years have added up to feminist consciousness—who shape history, or whether such figures are molded by the movement. Baker was herself an unjustly slighted prime mover in the movement who once worked for King, declaring of him after his death: "The movement made Martin rather than Martin making the movement." Scholar Richard Lischer disagrees with that assessment. He argues that the "Civil Rights Movement did not 'make' King any more than the Civil War 'made' Lincoln." Lischer acknowledges that like Lincoln "King was summoned by events he did not initiate and exposed to conditions he did not create, but his response was so powerful an *interpretation* of events that it reshaped the conditions in which they originated." King wasn't the first Negro to "champion the cause of civil rights," but he "was merely the first to name the struggle and to declare its meaning."

If King brilliantly named the struggle and declared its meaning, others have come along in the same messianic mold since his death to interpret the events and struggles of race—its progresses and retreats, its high moments and its utter embarrassments. While a lot has been written about King's leadership, not much has focused on King's views of black leadership and how they might help us view his major heir, Jesse Jackson, and to a lesser degree, Al Sharpton. Charismatic leadership of the sort that King embodied has many virtues. One of them is the ability to inspire the masses and to dramatize the push for equality. It has vices too; charismatic leaders often don't find useful ways to transfer power or transmit authority. Lethal forms of competition are the norm more than cooperation. And there is a need to consider a version of political leadership that combines charisma and formal institutional authority that challenges old-style racial leadership, best seen recently in the career of Barack Obama. Does his leadership fulfill King's vision or fall short?

King reflected intelligently on black leadership; those thoughts are useful in examining the achievements and character of representative leaders who've emerged in the post-King era. A discussion of King's flaws and weaknesses may also help move us past an idealization of his leadership and to appreciate the leadership of those who have found their voices in very different times than when King captivated the nation. And by doing so, perhaps we can appreciate that some of the same criticism lodged at present-day black leaders in the charismatic mode may have been aimed through them at King as well. These black Joshuas—a designation fraught with many complications and contradictions—have borne the burden of King's mantle, and have sought to claim or modify his legacy. Their gifts and limitations say a great deal about

what can be expected and achieved in the arena of race,
and say a lot about the role that black leaders play today.

When he was fresh to the field, King exulted in the
new age of race he saw on the national horizon. He felt
that such a revitalized era would be hastened by "intelligent, courageous and dedicated leadership." King wel-
comed the new period of change but called for "leaders
who are calm and yet positive, leaders who avoid the
extremes of 'hot-headedness' and 'Uncle Tomism.'" This
was more than a rhetorical flourish for King. It was the
application to race of one of King's favorite philosophical
methods: Hegel's dialectic, which involved stating a thesis, an antithesis, and then a synthesis that resolved the
tensions, and combined the best features, of opposites. But
the substance was just as important as the form. One must
neither be a hard-charging rebel without direction, thus
wasting precious racial resources, flying off each racial
handle in sight; nor a subversive figure whose racial calcu-
lations and gestures would sell out the race. Even so,
King's conscientious Hegelian maneuvering away from
the fatal compromises of the Uncle Tom couldn't prevent
him from wearing that title, acerbically given to him by
Malcolm X, just a few years later.

King also argued that "the urgency of the hour" calls
for leaders of "wise judgment and sound integrity—leaders
not in love with money, but in love with justice," leaders
"not in love with publicity, but in love with humanity,"
and leaders "who can subject their particular egos to the

greatness of the cause." Wisdom and integrity were key because the Negro cause was beginning to take off in exciting directions that demanded restraint and balance, and unimpeachable moral credentials. Negroes were often subject to a double standard, one that whites hardly noticed when applying rules to black life that they willfully ignored for themselves. Black folk had to pay attention to how they were being perceived in the white world as they pressed forward in the name of progress. The seductions of publicity were ubiquitous, but a particular trap for black leaders, because they could easily derail the interests of the race into blatant self-promotion. The black leader's ego, fed by too much praise and popularity, could be his downfall and that of his followers, and ultimately, the entire race. The virtues of justice and humility would ground the black leader; he would place the cause of the group above venal self-interest, avoiding the lure of cash that so easily silences the prophetic voice, a way of literally selling out. And he would constantly remember that his greatest role was to serve and uplift his brother and sister.

Several years later, King was even more insistent on principled black leadership. In explaining the white backlash to black progress in 1964, King placed the heaviest burden on white resistance, but he also took black leadership to task. King indicted black leaders as being "sporadic," sunk by leadership that "neither planned ahead nor maintained itself at the helm at all times." King may not have passed his own litmus test until he was a third of the way through the sixties. It wasn't until his Birmingham campaign that "King's idea of leadership" encompassed "the deliberate creation of new struggles or the conscious, advance selection of strategies and tactics." Before then, King's leadership style was molded by the spread of wisdom and the transmission of learning for black liberation. His leadership agenda was largely an improvisational affair, the creative management of a medley of themes and actions that were addressed as they arose. King would later seek to combine the best improvisational and intentional methods in his leadership efforts.

King's top-down bias shows through in the last part of his statement about leaders at the helm: in King's view, the black masses needed a constant and visible presence in charge to work and organize effectively. Even King's self-criticism—"All leaders, including myself, continued to work vigorously, but we failed to assert the leadership the movement needed"—plays into a leadership premised on hierarchy, even if in the name and interests of the black masses. Such a view slighted the efforts of the grassroots, and imposed a scheme and rationale that didn't always pay attention to the organic character of social change in local environments. For instance, King bumped heads with SNCC organizers in Albany, Georgia, because after their painstaking, local grassroots efforts, he rode into town to capture the spotlight and the credit for their hard work. Obviously even activists who spurned hierarchy wanted some recognition for their leadership—and for the hard work of the masses themselves in functioning as agents of their own freedom.

King argued that the vacuum created by the failure of legitimate leaders to step up and lead was filled by "less-experienced and frequently irresponsible elements." The response of the legitimate leaders was "either a negative reaction or disdain." Thus, irresponsible black leaders embarked on a "new, distorted form of action" that substituted "small, unrepresentative forces for the huge, mass, total-community movements" genuine black leaders had organized. For King, the purposes of mass demonstrations were to "isolate and expose the evildoer by the mass presence of his victims" and prove the Negro's unity to whites while making a case for concrete programs that could withstand scrutiny. But sporadic actions on the part of irresponsible groups disrupted the lives of blacks and their white allies. King cites the examples of a "mere handful of well-intentioned but tragically misguided young people" who when they blocked the "doorways to New York City's Board of Education, or threatened to stop traffic to the World's Fair, or charged into the streets to spread garbage, and to halt traffic on bridges . . . were reducing the imposing grandeur of the movement to cheap chaos." As a result, the "mass movement of millions was overnight exposed to ridicule and debasement."

King is clearly drawing distinctions between the mass demonstrations he led, which identified their targets and objectives—in Birmingham, Bull Connor's police force and the fight against segregation; in Selma, Sheriff Jim Clark and the right to vote—and the spurts of social rebellion by well-meaning but unfocused factions of youth. Such social gestures sullied the dignity of black protest. There may be more than a bit of paternalism in King's comments, or even a disdain for the organized chaos of social actions based on the philosophy of anarchy. King's words would come back to haunt him since his planned march on Washington in April of 1968 was feared to have the same anarchic effect.

In fact, King embraced disruption in his notion of aggressive nonviolence, though his version of mass civil disobedience was focused, massive, and sustained. King said that nonviolence had to be "adapted to urban conditions and urban moods," and that it must mature and "correspond to heightened black impatience and stiffened white resistance." King concluded that:

> There must be more than a statement to the larger society, there must be a force that interrupts its functioning at some key point . . . To dislocate the functioning of a city without destroying it can be more effective than a riot because it can be longer lasting, costly to the larger society, but not wantonly destructive. It is a device of social action more difficult for a government to quell by superior force . . . it is militant and defiant, not destructive.

King was careful to state twice that massive civil disobedience and aggressive nonviolence were not destructive. He earlier chided the "irritating deeds of certain irresponsible civil rights forces" because they were too often mistaken by the public as the "senseless violence" of Negro perpetrators, thus compromising the moral force of the civil rights movement. Civil rights leaders controlled the demonstrations they led and distinguished them from urban chaos and criminal acts by the discipline they exhibited. Still, the *Washington Post* concluded that King's planned act of massive social disruption of Washington, DC, with his Poor People's Campaign was "an appeal to anarchy." The *New York Times* editorialized that King invited disaster "in the present overheated atmosphere," and that his cause was damaged merely by announcing his plans "whether or not Dr. King goes ahead with his perilous project."

Despite his progressive views, King's "regal leadership image" made him vulnerable to criticism from grassroots and younger activists. At an SNCC private fund-raiser in New York in 1962, for which King had agreed to speak, host Harry Belafonte vigorously defended his friend to the SNCC cohort before he arrived. The students complained that King was too removed from the scene of struggle, that he was far too cautious, and that he was preoccupied with his fame. The example of SNCC leaders like Bob Moses—as modest a force for good as the movement produced, and an organizer who identified intimately with the folk—contrasted with King's comparatively glamorous and camera-hogging campaigns for justice. The younger activists argued that Belafonte's defense of King against their misguided criticisms drew from the entertainment credo that there should be a star for every show. When Belafonte insisted that King wasn't nearly as bourgeois as they made him out to be, the SNCC activists tore gleefully into King and his family: Coretta sported pearls and pillbox hats; his father, Daddy King, was imperiously self-centered; and King himself favored silk pajamas and nice vacations. The students admitted that Belafonte was right in insisting that no other leader would take their stern criticisms and still act with love. His admonishment was proved that evening when King spoke highly of the SNCC students and the lessons he learned from their sacrifices, while urging the audience to generously support them without mentioning his own SCLC.

What the younger activists probably didn't know is that King placed nearly all of his more than $200,000 yearly salary from speaking engagements into the civil rights till; that he refused to buy a home (because he strongly disagreed with private ownership of property) until his wife insisted in 1965; that he gave all of his book royalties to his alma mater, Morehouse College; and that he rotated a meager three suits near the end of his life in a spartan, guilt-driven leadership style that was witheringly self-critical and sacrificial. King's trusted aide and advisor Stanley Levison says that King was consumed with guilt over the kudos he got because he believed that he was simply "an actor in history at a particular moment that called for a personality, and he had simply been selected as that personality . . . but he had not done enough to deserve it." Levison says that King felt "keenly that people who had done as much as he had or *more* got no such tribute." King was "troubled deeply" about the praise he got that others should have received, but that there was little to be done since there's no way to share it with others. One had to accept it. He knew quite well from the Bible that many great men of calling felt intense discomfort in their role, but they had soldiered on in spite of their conflicted feelings. Levison argues that a conscientious man like King was haunted by his plight.

But when you don't feel you're worthy of it and you're an honest, principled man, it tortures you. And it could be said that he was tortured by the great appreciation that the public showed for him. If he had been less humble, he could have lived with this kind of acclaim, but because he was genuinely a man of humility, he really couldn't live with it. He always thought of ways in which he could somehow live up to it, and he often talked about taking a vow of poverty: getting rid of everything he owned—including his home—so that he could at least feel that nothing material came to him from his efforts.

Levison says that King's views were rooted in an awareness of his fortunate birth, and how he "was always aware that he was privileged . . . and this tortured him." Levison suggests one of "the reasons that he was so determined to be of service was to justify the privileged position he'd been born into." King felt that "he had never deserved and earned what he had," and that he didn't deserve the acclaim he received as a civil rights hero. "It was a continual series of blows to his conscience, and this kept him a very restive man all his life." King's brutal self-examination and relentlessly imposed self-sacrifice were nearly like Blaise Pascal's, the famous seventeenth-century philosopher, scientist, and mathematician whose ascetic Christianity contrasted to his privileged upbringing, and who, like King, died at thirty-nine years of age.

King's internal monologue may have run constantly in his brain, but it didn't shield him from accusations that his leadership was ineffective, particularly when he suffered a major defeat in the 1961–62 Albany campaign against segregation. King was outfoxed in Albany, Georgia, by Sheriff Laurie Pritchett, who was determined with Albany officials to manage demonstrations and the jailing of Negroes by meeting "nonviolence with nonviolence" and killing the demonstrators "with kindness." This strategy worked brilliantly; under King, the civil rights movement provoked often violent confrontations with governmental authorities to dramatize the brutality of the white oppressor in contrast to the nonviolent protesters. But Pritchett got the best of his civil rights opponents by refusing to take the bait of civil rights protest and instead matched their nonviolent efforts with a devilishly effective piece of preemptive policing. Since there was no violence or crisis—a deal was struck by local white and black leaders to postpone demonstrations and to free all demonstrators on bail, including King—the protest fizzled and King and the civil rights movement suffered one of its most visible and humiliating defeats. King was criticized for being "an absentee media star" and for "his failure to rely more heavily on the courts, his insensitivity to local whites," and "his reluctance to go to jail more frequently."

After Albany, King shunned the spotlight for eight months and licked his wounds as his name shrank to small newspaper print. He was viewed as a has-been freedom star from the fifties whose luster had dimmed and who had strained to become the kind of national leader that his talent simply couldn't sustain. King stung from the Albany criticism, but he learned too. Later, his 1963 campaign in Birmingham benefited from the flaws and faults in Albany. King scored one of the resounding victories of his leadership, and the civil rights movement, when the barbarism of Bull Connor was theatrically orchestrated to expose the vicious heart of Southern apartheid. As the

black activists, including women and children, assembled
to protest segregation, Connor directed his goons to spray
powerful water hoses on the marchers—when he wasn't
having police dogs sicced on them. Connor believed that
he was getting the upper hand against the protesters with
a dramatic show of brute force. But it backfired; instead of
being impressed by his reckless display, many politicians,
including the president, were appalled. The sight of water
hoses and police dogs unleashed on Negro demonstrators
was tailor-made for the evening news, prompting the president to act and Congress to pass the Civil Rights Bill.
King duplicated the feat in Selma, where violence reigned
and bloodshed poured—three activists died—helping to
win passage of the Voting Rights Bill in 1965.

King not only faced down intellectual criticism, and
the bluster and bile of Southern bigots, but he confronted
conflict with Northern black leaders as well. Adam Clayton Powell engaged in a turf war with King whenever the
Southern preacher lighted on New York City. Powell was
the powerful congressman from Harlem and, like King,
black church royalty as pastor of Abyssinian Baptist
Church. Butting heads was to be expected. Powell called
King a moderate who catered to "Whitey." Powell also
eventually threatened to expose King advisor Bayard
Rustin as a homosexual when Powell and King battled
over a boycott Rustin planned of the 1960 Democratic
National Convention in Los Angeles to pressure the party
to act on behalf of civil rights. The conflict forced Rustin

from the ranks of the SCLC. Rustin says that Powell warned King that "if he did not withdraw his support from the Rustin-led demonstration in Los Angeles, [Powell] would go to the press and say that there was a sexual affair going on between me and King. Martin was so terrified . . . he decided he would get rid of me."

In like fashion Rev. Joseph H. Jackson of Illinois, the imperial head of the National Baptist Convention, had King removed from his office as vice president of the Convention's Sunday School Board in 1961. The move was in retribution for King siding with Rev. Gardner Taylor in the dramatic effort to unseat the conservative, anti–civil rights Jackson as convention president. Jackson had originally won his position by demanding term limits, but when his final term came to a close, he reversed the amendment and won another four years. This violation of the convention's constitution was met with outrage by many of the members, including King, who with his father had originally helped put Jackson where he was. The schism between warring factions in the convention led to the secession of several pro–civil rights ministers, including King and Taylor, to form the Progressive National Baptist Convention.

But of all the Northern forces against him, King was most famously engaged in a war of words with Nation of Islam minister Malcolm X, whose stronghold was nestled in Harlem. King was critical of the separatist philosophy of the Black Nationalist group, while Malcolm mercilessly pelted King with epithets like "twentieth century Uncle Tom" and lashed him with the rejoinder that he was the "best weapon that the white man" ever had. King chafed under Malcolm's assault. He was bruised by Malcolm's claims about "my being soft and my talking about love and the white man all the time and . . . my being a sort of polished Uncle Tom." After he was deluged with eggs by Malcolm's followers on a trip to New York, King felt the need to "get my mind off of myself and feeling sorry for myself and feeling rejected." When Malcolm claimed that nonviolence made black folk weak and submissive, King replied that "I'm talking about a very strong force where you stand up with all our might against any evil system, and you're not a coward, you are resisting, but you come to see that tactically as well as morally it is better to be nonviolent." When King spoke out against the Vietnam War, he reaped a firestorm of opposition among prominent Negro leaders, figures, and intellectuals, from Carl Rowan to Jackie Robinson, and from Ralph Bunche to Roy Wilkins.

King's principled leadership also got him into trouble with the presidents who to varying degrees supported the civil rights movement. John F. Kennedy was tentative on civil rights, and ultimately didn't commit the necessary resources to push civil rights legislation through Congress. While Kennedy publicly praised King's "personal conduct and your dynamic leadership," which had earned "the respect and admiration of the great majority of the people of the United States," privately he fumed that should he give in to King's request for federal troops in Birmingham "it will look like he got me to do it." Kennedy offhandedly in private said that inviting King to the Oval Office during the tumult in Alabama was risky: "King is so hot these days that it's like having [Karl] Marx coming to the White House." And while Lyndon Baines Johnson worked diligently with King to push legislation through Congress and then sign the Civil Rights Bill and Voting Rights Act—key legal underpinnings to the quest for black equality—Johnson was enraged with King when he vocally opposed the Vietnam War in 1967, and privately cursed him. "What is that goddamned nigger preacher doing to me?" Johnson exploded in bitter bigotry. "We gave him the Civil Rights Act of 1964, we gave him the Voting Rights Act of 1965, we gave him the War on Poverty. What more does he want?" King never got inside the White House again.

Perhaps King engaged Kennedy and Johnson with such principled, though costly, interactions because of his strong views on the relationship between white patronage and subordinate black leadership. King argued that black political leaders must not imitate white leadership, especially in its condescending view of his own people.

Negro leaders suffer from . . . being either exalted excessively or grossly abused. Some of these leaders suffer from an aloofness and absence of faith in their people. The white establishment is skilled in flattering and cultivating emerging leaders. It presses its own image on them and finally, from imitation of manners, dress and style of living, a deeper strain of corruption develops. This kind of Negro leader acquires the white man's contempt for the ordinary Negro. He is often more at home with the middle-class white than he is among his own people. His language changes, his location changes, his income changes, and ultimately he changes from the representative of the Negro to the white man into the white man's representative to the Negro. The tragedy is that too often he does not recognize what has happened to him.

King was highly critical of the white cultural mechanisms that promoted Negro political leadership within black culture, saying that the powers that be exploited the manner in which black leadership emerged. King argued a year before his death that the "majority of Negro political leaders do not ascend to prominence on the shoulders of mass support." He conceded that genuine leaders were emerging, but that "most are still selected by white leadership, elevated to position, supplied with resources and inevitably subjected to white control." King said that most Negroes had a healthy skepticism about the "manufactured leader" because he expends little effort in convincing them of his integrity, commitment, and ability. Plus, he offers paltry programs and service. Such a leader is not "a fighter for a new life but a figurehead of the old one." King concluded that few Negro politicians were impressive and had little support in black circles.

King argued that the status of these Negro leaders prevented them from effectively bargaining with the white power structure with strength and independence. White political leaders treated a black political leader with little real regard because of his "impotence" and his distance from his constituents, viewing him as a "powerless subordinate." Since the Negro politician had no real base or firm footing in either black or white society, he was stuck in a vacuum with no influence or leverage. Thus, the Negro had to create moral black leaders who could gain black confidence. But such support was not automatic; the politics of pigment and color were insufficient to win black approval. Blacks "will have to demand high standards and give consistent, loyal support to those who merit it" and who "prove themselves to be committed political warriors on our behalf." Only when black folk developed "partisan political personalities whose independence is genuine" would they "be treated in white political councils with the respect those who embody such power deserve."

King's leadership was a powerful combination of the Hegelian opposites he embraced. Many times, he was more progressive than was customary in American politics (he argued for a reconstruction of American society and a radical redistribution of wealth to the poor) and yet he could be cautious and moderate—and sometimes conservative

(August Meier called him the "militant conservative"). King could be decisive and focused, while at other times he could be indecisive, unfocused, paralyzed, and unsure of where to head. King was perhaps the most self-effacing prominent black leader ever, and yet there were flashes of conscious mythmaking around his own image in the spotlight of the media. But the cumulative impact of King's leadership is perhaps discerned in a story King told in a 1967 *New York Times Magazine* article to illustrate the ideal black leader.

Two men flew to Atlanta to meet with a black leader at the airport. But before they spoke, a porter sweeping the floor engaged the black leader about a troubling personal issue. After fifteen minutes of conversation between the leader and the porter, one of the visitors complained bitterly to his fellow visitor that he was too busy for such nonsense, that he hadn't come a thousand miles to sit and wait while the leader spoke to a porter. But the other visitor replied, "When the day comes that he stops having time to talk to a porter, on that day I will not have the time to come one mile to see him." King was as good as his illustration: when he was on the way in to a crucial staff meeting in the last year of his life, he paused to speak to a janitor about his wife's illness, spending more than forty-five minutes in compassionate conversation as his staff waited.

Despite King's charismatic leadership, within his organization he encouraged his staff, likened to a team of wild horses, to run free, engage in vigorous debate, offer tough, direct criticism of King's ideas—all while King listened. King depended upon Andrew Young to chart the conservative path to Jesse Jackson's, Hosea Williams's, and James Bevel's more radical suggestions so that King could "come down the middle." King displayed his extraordinary security, and his appreciation of others' gifts, in his leadership style. But on very rare occasions he could also be quite harsh. In a meeting with some of his aides, including SCLC executive director William Rutherford, and with Stokely Carmichael, Courtland Cox, and SNCC chairman H. Rap Brown, King met to get the black nationalists to agree to not interfere with—or taint with violence—SCLC's Poor People's Campaign efforts in DC. Cox pledged that, while they couldn't support the march, they would neither oppose it nor keep black folk from helping each other. Rutherford deemed Cox's reply reasonable, but King disagreed, insisting that a genuine commitment to nonviolence meant that no destructive forms of action could be tolerated, regardless of their purpose. As the meeting broke up, King did an extremely rare thing: he lambasted Rutherford in public. "Dr. King never ever humiliated anyone in public in front of anyone else," Rutherford remembered. "But he was *shaking*." Rutherford concluded that King wasn't so much speaking to him, but to himself and history. He read King's fit of rage as a sign of just how exhausted he was, and just how poorly the Poor People's Campaign was going.

In the last week of his life, King gave members of his staff a brutal rebuff. King was in a meeting in Atlanta listening to his staff trash the idea of his Poor People's March, and even the usually reliable Andrew Young teamed up with Jesse Jackson and James Bevel to oppose the late-April march to DC. Young argued that the poor planning for the march might push it back a year, while questioning the wisdom of assembling masses of the poor in DC. Bevel insisted that instead of "hanging around Washington," they needed "to stop this war." And Jackson called the Memphis mobilization too small and Washington too unformed, and since there was no timetable for how long they'd be in DC, it made no sense to pull away from the successful negotiations with big corporations and youth gangs being conducted by Operation Breadbasket. King replied to all three that whenever they needed his aid with their individual projects, he was there for them, and now all he was asking for was their help. And then, King "did something I've never heard him do before," said Stanley Levison. "He criticized three members of the staff with his eloquence. And believe me, that's murder. And was very negative." King let loose with calm accusations against all three, claiming that they all had given in to different forces: Young to doubt, Bevel to brains, and Jackson to ambition. All three, King claimed, had forgotten the need to bear witness, and now that the movement had made them, they were each using the movement for self-promotion. King scolded Bevel, who'd been Young's and Jackson's mentor: "You don't like to work on anything that isn't your own idea. Bevel, I think you owe *me* one."

When Abernathy, Jackson, and Young ran after King, who had demanded that Abernathy hand him his car keys, it was Jackson who sought to soothe King's ruffled feathers in the stairwell as King departed. "Doc, doc, don't worry!" Jackson called to his boss and mentor. "Everything's going to be all right."

But King would have none of it this time, and uncharacteristically wheeled around on a landing and raised his hands and pointed at Jackson while shouting. "Jesse, everything's *not* going to be all right! If things keep going the way they're going now, it's not SCLC but the whole country that's in trouble. I'm not asking, 'Support me.' I don't need this. But if you're so interested in doing your own thing that you can't do what this organization's structured to do, if you want to carve out your niche in society, go ahead. But for God's sake, don't bother me!" King's rage resounded in the Atlanta staff building's conference room.

Of course, to a degree, King was justified in his frustration with the trio. They chipped away at him, perhaps exploiting King's tolerance of what might in other quarters be perceived as disrespect and insubordination. King's last interaction with Jackson after the staff meeting has marked the younger man's career, a touchstone of mythology that suggests his lethal ambition, a millstone that was hung around his neck even before he began his meteoric flash to fame. King's judgment of Jackson has been inscribed on him like a walking epitaph; instead of burying him, however, King's remarks the week before he died simply catapulted Jackson to stratospheric heights. In the forty years since King's death, it is Jackson who has best captured his mentor's spirit, extended his work, and interpreted his vision as the most prominent and powerful black leader in the post-King era.

# CHAPTER
# EIGHT

## HEIR APPARENT

THE IMAGE THAT LAUNCHED JESSE JACKSON in the public mind was drenched in mythology and his mentor's blood. After King's assassination, Ralph Abernathy, Andrew Young, and other aides accompanied his body to the hospital while other staff members lingered at the motel's courtyard trying to make sense of their leader's demise. Jesse Jackson stayed behind and spoke to the press, which began arriving around 6:25 p.m., less than a half hour after King was shot. In speaking to the press, Jackson seemed to break the very rule he had just barked out to an associate. "Jesse called to me from across the lot and said, 'Don't talk to them!'" said Ben Branch, the musician King had requested to play "Precious Lord, Take My Hand," who was also the music director of Operation Breadbasket's band. "I agreed because I thought he meant none of us were supposed to talk until Abernathy got back from the hospital. So I walked away."

As Jackson spoke to a television reporter, Hosea Williams listened in and didn't like what he heard. "I heard Jesse say, 'Yes, I was the last man in the world King spoke to.' I knew Jesse was lying because Solomon Jones was the one, and I had a feeling about what Jesse was trying to pull. I climbed over the railing and was going to stomp him into the ground but a cop grabbed me. I called Jesse a dirty, stinking, lying so-and-so . . . I had no hang-ups about Jesse talking to the press. That was okay, but why lie? Why capitalize on another man's name and image—a dead man, who can't speak for himself?" (Writer Gary Wills was in Memphis shortly after King's death and reported that "SCLC members who have denounced Jackson for his publicity seeking—Hosea Williams, especially, and James Bevel—were very aggressive in their courting of the cameras in the next few days." Perhaps Williams was mad that Jackson beat him to the punch.) Many news outlets repeated the story that Jackson was the last man to whom King spoke and that he had cradled the dying leader in his arms, getting his blood all over him. That account has fueled the mythological passing of the leadership mantle from King to Jackson, a neatly staged succession story designed to legitimate Jackson's standing as what *Playboy* magazine a little more than a year later called the "fiery heir apparent to Martin Luther King."

The moment of Jackson's emergence is shadowed with conflicting reports. It seems that the staff agreed in an emergency meeting the night of King's murder not to speak with the press, more than likely to show unity and to exhibit the movement imperative to control the message. Jackson was absent, excused by Abernathy to return to Chicago to organize planeloads of people to attend King's funeral, although Hosea Williams remembers Jackson telling him he was ill and needed to see his physician for medicine. In any event, Jackson turned up the next day to speak at a special meeting of the Chicago City Council and, before that, in the morning on NBC's *Today Show,* wearing on both occasions the same bloody shirt he had on when he last saw the prophet on that desolate balcony of destiny, which now became a ledge of opportunity for the ambitious protégé.

Jackson's actions provoked the consternation of his fellow acolytes. They questioned his claim that he was on the balcony at all since he was in the courtyard when the report rang out and slammed King to the ground. But a famous picture of King's associates pointing in the direction of the sniper's bullet, with what appears to be Jackson's figure partially masked by a woman, bears out his contention that he was there. He had obviously climbed the stairs in the commotion to be by King's body. As for the claim that he cradled King in his arms, most of those around the scene initially denied it, but how to explain the blood on Jackson's shirt?

"I can see Jesse going over and leaning down and placing both his palms down flat in that pool of blood, and then standing up and . . . wiping down the front of his shirt," Andrew Young now admits. Neither was Jackson the only one to crave King's blood; after returning from the hospital, Abernathy produced a jar and began scraping King's blood up with the cardboard from a laundered shirt, crying, "This is Martin's precious blood. This blood was shed for us." Young says that there's "nothing that unusual about [Jackson's gesture], it's what you'd have done. We Baptists, you know, we believe there's power in the blood—power that's transferable." Jackson endured the trauma of losing his leader by becoming him, or at least, getting as close as his admiring imitation could bring him until he, in his own clothes and voice, became the leader he always longed to be. In the meantime, Jackson's naked bid for succession as King's heir apparent was fueled by internal demons and a stunning self-confidence, even self-importance, that had driven him long before his public career began.

Jackson was born in 1941 in Greenville, South Carolina, as an illegitimate son to a teen mother—sired by a former professional boxer and married man who lived next door to her parents. Jackson grew up under a cloud of controversial paternity back when such births carried a stigma now hard to imagine, especially when films like *Juno* and *Knocked Up* challenge societal norms as much as reflect them. Jackson was mercilessly teased by his mates as he matured. He took his revenge in besting his better off peers by becoming the president of everything and by working harder than everyone else to enhance his native intellectual gifts. He also consoled himself in the cool winds of achievement that hugged him. It was the sense of being delegitimated and decertified that pushed Jackson higher and harder.

Though his mother married when he was two, it would be twelve years before his stepfather officially adopted him, and his illegitimacy gave him a grudge against mediocrity and invisibility. It swore him to a Protestant work ethic to outdo his socially established competitors in the iron-cage world of segregated black America where the black elite were forced to breathe the same air as their less fortunate kin. If segregated black America was hardly the mixture of social altruism and cohesion now popular in nostalgic accounts of black life under Jim Crow, the classes nevertheless forged paths in the same schools and churches, barbershops and haberdasheries. The well-to-do got a sense of the pluck and pride of their lesser kin while the poor got a sense of the material possibilities that lay ahead for those who strived to exceed their parents' limitations.

Jackson was denied standing in the world into which King was born. Jackson pressed his nose against the glass barriers that kept King safe and nurtured, whether in fine stores or the homes of the black elite. What King could gather at his parents' table—a sense of self bigger than the prejudice that obscured black achievement—Jackson had to gather in schools from teachers used to spotting talented students. The stability that comes from having a father at home, even an overbearing one like King's father, eluded Jackson, grating at his ego, chafing his pride, and scraping his sense of somebodyness. It forced him to flex back in reaction against degrading, denying forces, driving him to overcompensate for his loss. Except his loss was even more painful because he got a view of what could have been his as he witnessed the legitimacy and comfort of his half-brother, Noah. Years later, when he poured forth in dramatic cadence "I am somebody . . . I may be poor, but I am somebody," he had to look no further than the mirror to catch a glimpse of his natural constituency.

Even King recognized the effects of father-deprivation on Jackson—although Jackson's stepfather, Charles Jackson, gave him affection and offered his family care and protection. But it could never adequately compensate for the hidden injuries and psychic bruises that unleashed in Jackson a rage for acceptance and one-upmanship. Excellence was both the compensation for hard work and the way to defeat the defeaters. King had a complicated relationship with Jackson: he initially frowned on Abernathy's choice to bring the twenty-three-year-old into the SCLC fold. But his helpfulness at the Selma campaign, where Jackson went to volunteer and to seek a job with King, endeared him to Abernathy, who would act as a sort of mentor to Jackson. It would be especially bitter for Abernathy's friends when, after King's death, Jackson set out to eclipse him as the heir apparent to King and the leader of black folk.

Once his initial reservations were placated, King readily spotted Jackson's enormous talents and moved quickly to name Jackson head of the Chicago Division of SCLC's Operation Breadbasket in 1965. Operation Breadbasket was developed to hold businesses accountable that had exploited black folk by accepting their patronage while denying them jobs. Breadbasket countered this discrimination with selective buying and economic boycotts against those businesses, as well as those that refused to purchase goods and services from black contractors. Jackson would become the national face of Operation Breadbasket in 1966, running it from his base in Chicago.

King also astutely gauged Jackson's outsize ambitions: his hunger to help, his desire to lead. Andrew Young says that Jackson's "willingness to assume responsibility" in Selma in the march from Selma to Montgomery distinguished him from other Northern students. Young didn't realize at the time that Jackson had been a veteran of Greensboro's student movement. His impressions of Jackson were favorable:

Tall and handsome, Jesse had an air of confidence and was willing to take the initiative. He had proved himself to be responsible and levelheaded in Selma and, unlike the SNCC students, Jesse did not have a romance with the proletariat: while SNCC was striving for a nonleadership model and saw themselves as anti-authoritarian facilitators, Jesse's model for leadership was the traditional Baptist preacher. He was eager for the leadership mantle. We didn't know exactly what was driving Jesse, but Martin appreciated Jesse's desperate desire to lead and encouraged it.

Young says that he "always suspected that Jesse's childhood as the son of a single mother created in him a constant psychological need for a father figure." He says that Jackson's "leadership drive was a product of that need for attention and approval," and that as a student, he "seemed drawn to the glory of leadership and looked to Martin as a paternal authority." Young says that while neither he nor King "had any trouble being a brother to Jesse, we were struggling ourselves with our own identity development and in no position to play a fatherly role."

King was often the recipient of Jackson's ability to spit a stream of rhetoric that sometimes overwhelmed the slower, gentler, less animated King. On some occasions Jackson was so eager to engage and impress King that he pelted him with questions only to answer himself before his mentor had time to respond. Jackson idolized King, loved the way he stood bravely for black people, loved his oratorical magic, and admired how he loved black people enough to die for them. Jackson may well have longed to be where King was and to do what he did—not out of jealousy, but out of a burning desire to share his gifts with the movement. King knew of Jackson's undisciplined grasp for leadership; the young man's hunger for vindication melded with his yen to change the world at a pace that matched the whirling demons inside him. It reflected the desire of all young Turks to seize the times by the throat and to coax change in newer, more slashing idioms. King's language resounded less shrilly in the terms of moral revolution.

When King was killed, Jackson acted immediately to seize the reins of leadership, to square his internal ambition with his external status. He found the right opportunity to ascend as his leader and elder brother lay on the ground, not yet cold. Before King was buried, Jackson was planning to pitch himself as King's successor. His ability to cut through the thicket of events surrounding King's assassination and to focus on microphones and television cameras to interpret King's death, and attach himself to King's legacy, was conniving, self-serving—and race-saving, redeeming, and the expression of a nearly inevitable trajectory of ascent that King himself had predicted. King had half-jokingly warned his staff that they had better be careful lest young Jackson ended up leading them one day.

Jackson's bloody shirt and media mastery suggest a religious use of death and blood to sanctify a movement, to secure a legacy—King's and Jackson's—and to point to a successor who was appointed by the leader. If Jackson dipped his hands into the blood of the prophet, it proved

he was both calculating *and* a good Christian. Jackson
understood the disciples symbolically drank the blood of
Jesus to memorialize his death; he merely tailored that
theology to himself and to black America in the loss of
their messiah. After all, King had accepted the messianic
role thrust on him as humbly as he could, taking the
good—the elevation by his people to a status near Jesus—
and the bad—risking his life and paying with his body
and blood to secure the redemption of his people and
nation. Jackson could hardly be blamed for doing his part
to usefully exploit King's messianic stature, even if it split
the difference between self-promotion and group edifica-
tion, a compromise Jackson would constantly be accused
of making. The racial transubstantiation, the holy Eucha-
rist of the blood of King, and his body, too, could be broken and shared, drank and consumed, as energizing rituals
of solidarity and sanctification, of sacred remembrance. If
Jackson was the wisest and most handy liturgist, it made
sense that it was precisely at the point of death that he
should spring to life—to more fully grasp the meaning of
King's mission, and the uses of his death. If King didn't
consciously pass along his mantle to Jackson—in fact, if
he withheld it deliberately, punitively, or suspiciously, as
if it were his to give in the first place, as if by wishing he
could boost Abernathy beyond his talents, or by warning
he could keep Jackson from his portion—Jackson nevertheless believed it was his to have. Such a belief reveals
both undisturbed hubris and unshakable confidence,

appearing to be the result of vulgar scheming and at the same time, feeling utterly natural and, finally, almost necessary and inexorable.

Thus, objections to the manner in which Jackson gained power are almost beside the point. Jackson's leadership abilities were greater, his inspirational skills more staggering, his speaking gifts bigger, his ego more massive, and his hunger to be the vessel of change deeper than all the rest of King's men. If he hadn't arranged to get there, he would have almost certainly been pushed to the top by the cycles of fate, fortune, luck, ambition, and the size of his sight and fight. When it came to his capacity to dream himself beyond his circumstances, Jackson's eyes were never bigger than his gut, and with pugilist genes at his command, he was more than ready for the fight. Besides, it couldn't have been his desire alone that got him there. Many others wanted it just as much in their own way, but he was the most talented among those who wanted it badly; although, it must be noted, wanting it badly is a necessary but insufficient basis for assuming charismatic leadership. When it came down to it, Jackson simply had what it took to present himself as the heir to Martin Luther King Jr. Still, Jackson couldn't trust that his talent alone would land him in the driver's seat. He had seen the bourgeois set get over because they were lighter, or better educated, or had better pedigree. The same qualities he would later display *as* leader had to be applied to the process to *become* leader: he had to outthink, outfox, outcalculate, outstrategize, and outwork all others in the field.

As for Jackson's succession scenario, it is almost always assumed that King's measure of Jackson's ambition and plans was benign, and remarkably, for the most part, that's true—but not absolutely. King praised Jackson for his hard work, and even quoted him in the last speech he gave in Memphis. King lauded Jackson's good qualities, but he also smelled Jackson's impatient, imperious drive, his approaching footsteps, all of which added up to successor and competitor. "Just be patient, Jesse," King said to him. "Your time will come." Others sensed Jackson's hunger for the premier spot. "I think Jesse wanted to be *the* number one black American leader himself someday. Now I don't think Jesse was foolish enough to believe that he could displace King. But he was clearly competing with him anyway." If the person in question has no real talent, is no real threat, then such desires can be abided. King was more patient than most because even when the threat was real, he still tolerated the hoofbeats of largely friendly competition from Jackson. King perhaps spotted before anyone else the real capacity for leadership that Jackson possessed. Perhaps King was agitated that someone could so nakedly want to wear a crown that King didn't think he himself deserved to wear. Perhaps it was his sense that anyone who hadn't yet earned the right to rise should simply not covet an elevated perch. Perhaps King sensed that Jackson's unbridled ambitions would harm the movement.

Perhaps he wanted to spare Jackson the drama and burden of leadership that he had no idea he was asking himself into. Perhaps it was his sense that Jackson was not yet ready, that even his gargantuan talents couldn't bring him to resist the nasty tide the movement was taking.

Or maybe King felt, or feared, that Jackson's brand of leadership might be the way to go, or that, should the people be exposed to him they would feel that way, rightly or wrongly—and that despite his big ego and need for recognition, his ideas and style were more suited to a younger generation surging to the fore. Jackson physically towered over King; he was a strikingly handsome figure, tall and full of sex appeal in a way that King wasn't. Of course, the young Jackson was already full of himself. When he and King arrived once at a mass meeting, Jackson says he refrained from speaking when "he noticed how the young people in the crowd got all excited when they saw [Jackson]. So he decided he would take a backseat, because he didn't want to take anything away from Dr. King."

One observer says that "Jesse's grabbing at the leadership became a big problem for them. King never showed consternation, but Andy Young was visibly perturbed." Young admits that all the men surrounding King went through a similar phase of thinking they could best King at leadership because he was so mild-mannered and humble. "Typically, brash young men mistake humility for weakness, and everybody was always doing that to

Martin—thought they could one-up him, manipulate him, co-opt him for their own purposes," Young says. "And he'd never fight back." Still, Young believed that Jackson over-stepped even that boundary. For instance, at the opening mass rally for SCLC's Chicago campaign at Soldier Field, Jackson's naked ambition "really shook us," Young says. "This was supposed to be Dr. King's moment. The only thing was, Jesse was speaking earlier in the program, and he tried to do an imitation of the March on Washington speech. I mean, it was obvious he was trying to do a Dr. King speech himself, not a speech as just a director of the Chicago project. He was trying to give his *own* vision for the movement in the future. It just wasn't *appropriate*."

Jackson was driven as well by having finally gained access—after being excluded for most of his life—to the black middle-class circles that King frequented as a youth, circles of power and protection, and of social privilege. King had by then committed class suicide in his radical identification with the poor, but it was a noble choice that still rested on privilege: he had the psychic wherewithal and the emotional security from having been a member of the black elite to cast his fate with the downtrodden. Though it may be hard to surrender privilege—and the numbers of the fortunate who don't voluntarily do it tes-tify to this fact—it is still easier to give up what one had than actively spurn the privilege one has never tasted.

While it's true that King refused to brazenly exploit his status as the greatest civil rights leader, he could also afford to be humble because the world proclaimed him a god. There were also corners to King's psyche, and moments when he understandably, humanly, rejected his humble demeanor, which escaped public notice. Writer David Halberstam caught one of them in his 1967 essay on King for *Harper's* magazine.

> King is a frustrating man. Ten years ago, *Time* found him humble, but few would find him that way today, though the average reporter coming into contact with him is not exactly sure why; he suspects King's vanity. One senses that he is a shy and sensitive man thrown into a prominence which he did not seek but which he has come to accept, rather likes, and intends to perpetuate. Colleagues find him occasionally pretentious . . . He has finally come to believe his myth, just as the people in the Pentagon believe theirs and the man in the White House believes his; he sticks to the morality of his life and of his decisions, until there becomes something of a mystic quality to him.

King's good friend and legendary pulpiteer Samuel Proctor said that "I'm not sure that King was not aware of this sense of destiny. Every now and then, I'd hear something drop from his lips. I'll never forget hearing him say, 'I have wondered how long I should have kept my silence on the Vietnam question.' Kind of like, you know, the whole world has only been waiting for you to break your silence." Proctor says that "phrases like that he'd let fall" with increasing frequency. Another friend recalls how King responded to a 1963 *Newsweek* poll that confirmed King as the most popular black leader among black people. "Martin got up and rushed to the nearest newsstand. He had that copy of *Newsweek* already opened to the poll. He kept looking at it, and after a while, he must have sensed that I thought it was all disgusting, so he closed up the magazine. He pretended to be contrite. He said, 'I know I shouldn't care what they think about me. I just ought to pay it no mind and do what I must. I shouldn't be so vain.' But he was feeling good because he was first." This may be why King could preach so effectively and brilliantly about the "drum major instinct"; he felt its lure inside his own breast.

King warred mightily against his vanity in a way that never occurred to Jesse Jackson. Perhaps he was so hard on Jackson because he knew more than most how seductively the sirens of fame could beckon. King probably knew, as one aide put it, that "Jesse could never pass a reflective surface without pausing—whether it was a store window or just a shiny car, he'd have to stop a second and check himself out again." But King loved Jackson and understood him much better than Jackson's fellow staffers who were irritated by his desperate need for affirmation from King and others. "You're very lucky you had both a mother and daddy who loved you," King told his staff, "and so you don't compulsively need attention. Jesse compulsively needs attention." King also confessed to aides that "Jesse's just so independent, so ambitious." Once, when King looked at a *Jet* magazine photo of Jackson that had been supplied by his Operation Breadbasket office—where Jackson was standing in a pulpit with a portrait of King beneath him and a cross hanging high behind him—he said, "Well, at least he had the good grace to place himself below the Savior."

What King may have not fully acknowledged is that when others lift you up high, it is far easier to practice humility. There is a paradoxical element of high self-regard in self-debasement, as if one is specially singled out by destiny or divinity to sacrifice and suffer. King grappled with that paradox as he received the praise of the masses. Jackson, however, was a one-man team, at least at the beginning of his career; he had no one else to rely on but himself. Even if God was on his side, he'd still have to do most of the heavy lifting, since King had most of the "God has ordained you to this task" talk on lock. Jackson had to work overtime to be both cheerleader for King and self-booster—though surely being in place to champion King had its advantages. One could be *seen* and *heard* shaking the pompoms for King, and thus, indirectly, one was cheerleading and boosting oneself.

With Jackson's star on the ascendant even as King's was beginning to dim in the backlash to his positions on war and poverty, it is not unreasonable to believe that King felt some unpleasant pressure, perhaps even resentment, in Jackson's relentless striving. He certainly couldn't have been deaf to the rumblings of Jackson's increasingly superior effect on people. Dorothy Collins, a former *Chicago Today* woman's editor, said to her coworkers after hearing Jackson, "King gave a hell of a speech, but you should have heard that kid, Jesse." And attorney Anna Langford, who would become Chicago's first black female alderwoman, said that "after I heard that kid speak, I felt that all the rest of the Breadbasket speakers could go home—including King." No matter how humble, how self-denying, there is something in the ego that, like nature, abhors a vacuum created by one's increasing absence, especially when that absence is, even if gently or subtly, being actively sought. The times were reversing King's formula for change, and in body and spirit, Jackson was King in reverse: King could afford to be calm, patient, humble, self-effacing. Jackson was driven to compensate for the lack of recognition; hence, exposure was the key to his psyche and soul's development—and his manner of being and leading. Even the acronym for the group he would later form upon heated departure from the SCLC would sum up his drive and testify to his style and ambition: PUSH.

These undercurrents also suggest that there was a bit of unconscious revenge that took place when Jackson snatched from King's grave and his not-yet-cold-body the mantle of leadership. King's last words to Jackson, which stung him deeply, had been a particularly harsh rebuke for

his fatal ambition. In adopting a critical posture toward
Jackson, King may have conjured the image of the black
elite finding fault with him. King stood in for the very
black bourgeoisie he had in many ways rejected as he
expressed scorn for Jackson's ambition and style. In grasp-
ing King's legacy, even in the face of King's desire to see it
transmitted to Abernathy, Jackson was getting a kind of
revenge on the black bourgeoisie who judged him. Jackson was getting a leg up on the privileged and educated
who kept him out, who were suspicious of him, although
King and Young nobly forsook their comfortable upbring-
ings to give their lives to the movement. Jackson's
revenge, or his sweetly poetic justice, was complete after
he rose to become the most significant black leader after
King's death.

Although he has prestige and responsibility as King's
most noted apostle, Jackson's leadership has in many ways
proved him as the anti-King, or at least, the un-King.
Gone in Jackson is the ravaging guilt that shredded
King's psyche in three: remorse for cheating on his wife;
guilt over being featured as the H.N.I.C. (head Negro in
charge); and sorrow over not serving God and man suffi-
ciently. By contrast, there was, especially as a young black
leader, a defiant swagger in Jackson, an athlete's bold
self-possession: the confidence of the utterly black-and-
beautiful. And with the rise of a black power esthetic that
Jackson embraced, his youthful Afro was the bane of the
bourgeoisie, and a sign of self-acceptance to the brothers

and sisters in the streets who struggled for self-recognition. Jackson's Black Nationalist, and at other times, ghetto country getup—dashikis and denim in smooth sartorial rotation, and neck medallions and cowboy boots too, and turtlenecks and suede sports jackets—were the garb and accessories of his outcast spiritual shamanism. His wardrobe signified both street mesmerism and ministerial charisma, a symptom of the black working class's excommunication from privileged black circles. Jackson became an accessible icon for its grievances with black *and* white elites.

If Martin Luther King had to decamp on the hood as a sign of ultimate class suicide—renouncing the privilege of his bourgeois upbringing to solidify his standing as a ghetto saint—Jackson was a ghetto superstar, a native of the projects who poured his bravura and his grievance through his syrupy thick speech. Jackson's words winced and winked in the battle against white supremacy, even as he returned fire with every weapon in his impressive rhetorical arsenal: gutbucket metaphors, urban parables, extended analogies, street slang, country grammar, theological sophistication, Southern diction, preacherly pacing, biting wit and humor, and an imperishable will to clarity. Jackson made love in language; he relished promiscuous verbal trysts with audiences around the world, flexing and undulating and twisting his meanings in an erotically agitated cadence that conjured the spirit and the flesh in the same breath. His rhyming speech was

an unavoidable homage to Muhammad Ali and a forerunner to hip hop, as Jackson played rebel badass and
strutting reverend with equal vigor. Jackson's verbal vitae
also tentatively resolved in style what couldn't be bridged
in philosophy or in person: Malcolm X's slashing and
combative rhetorical fusillade and the high elegance of
King's most finely wrought phrasing. Jackson also combined King's analytical sharpness with Abernathy's colorful down-home vernacular to offer engaging snapshots of
the black condition.

"How many of you watch those cowboy movies on
TV?" Jackson asked his regular Saturday morning gather-
ing at Operation Breadbasket in 1969. "They're a lesson
y'all got to learn. At first there ain't nothin' on the scene
but pistols and money. Bang! Bang! A man holds up the
stagecoach. Who has the most power? The man with the
most money. He can be so ugly he looks like he's been
made in a Headstart program and it doesn't matter.

"Now the rich man starts building up his economic
base. Opens a saloon or a general store. Then he brings in
the law. For justice? To make him give the money back?
Course not. The law's there to make sure no one robs the
rich man. He's the legislature, not only protects but
decides who gets protected.

"Next the schoolmarm gets off the stagecoach. She
interprets history and teaches culture. Since the rich man
already has his money, he wants everybody else to be
polite.

"Finally the preacher comes to town and forgives the rich man his original sin. Old folks who stole money start getting scared.

"That's how you go about forming a civilization. First the economic base, then the legislature to protect it—that's politics—then the culture to interpret it, finally religion to justify it. Y'all understand what I'm telling you? Say amen."

Since his early days in the spotlight, Jackson has become one of the most gifted public moralists, and public intellectuals, in the nation. Martin Luther King's brilliance was certified in having received a PhD in theology from Boston University. By contrast, Jackson didn't receive his master of divinity degree from Chicago Theological Seminary—which he left in 1965 after King promised him that six months working with him would be worth six years in school—until 2000. King has come under fire for plagiarism in large portions of his academic work, and some of his written and spoken work, since leaving Boston University. Some critics have argued that King's doctorate be rescinded; others claim he was an intellectual fraud. But no one who ever encountered King's lively mind on stage or in public conversation where he called upon his huge reserve of knowledge could doubt his intellectual pedigree.

But King's posthumous troubles only accent how remarkable are Jackson's considerable intellectual gifts. From the beginning of his time with King and SCLC,

Jackson showed a deep intellectual hunger and unquenchable curiosity that sometimes proved daunting even to the
formidably brilliant King. On a trip to Atlanta for his
first SCLC staff meeting, Jackson and fellow white semi-
narian David Wallace stayed with King at his home
because they lacked money for food and lodging. Jackson
smothered King in relentless intellectual dialogue "in
which he'd ask King a question and then answer it himself," Wallace says. "Because Jesse thinks while he talks,
you know. We were flying once from Atlanta to Savannah
for a retreat, and the whole flight down, Jesse is sitting
by King, with these books he'd been reading in his lap,
Tillich and Niebuhr, and asking King questions about
them like some hyper student, and then answering the
questions himself as he thought through them in asking
them. Until King finally said, 'Well Jesse, you don't even
give me time to answer the question.'" This bothered
King's staff, but King was usually tolerant, though on one
occasion he became so exasperated that he bluntly
instructed his protégé to leave him alone. "Don't send me
away, Doc," Jackson pleaded, "don't send me away."

It may be that Jackson's intense personality—even
then, other aides to King say, he was always "on," a trait
he hasn't lost in the last forty years—and his equally ravenous intellectual appetite make him the most original
thinker to emerge from civil rights circles. King brilliantly borrowed and synthesized ideas in responding to
critical social and moral issues. Jackson, lacking King's

formal education, was forced to think for himself, improvising and inventing answers from the depth of his intellectual energy and the vast reach of his curiosity about the world around him. His native intelligence and skills, and his willingness to do the difficult work of thinking deeply and independently, in alliance with his Herculean work ethic, make him a formidable public intellectual. His speeches and interviews shine with brilliant interpretations and teem with ideas and information.

In 1969, Jackson told *Playboy* magazine that poor whites held fast to their racist views at peril to their identification with poor black people that recalls W. E. B. Du Bois's analysis of how poor whites clung to the "psychic wages of whiteness" against their self-interest. "The white poor have always been distracted from demanding their rights; they've been too embarrassed to admit their deprivation. They've nourished themselves on the meager psychic diet of racism . . . United in a class struggle, we can force the redistribution of wealth in America." Earlier in the interview Jackson weighed in on how black progress wasn't nearly as significant as the progress of white society. "The economy quadruples while blacks creep along with unemployment as high as 35 and 40 percent in some black communities. When the white unemployment rate was 20 percent in 1933, it was a Depression that required massive aid. But the black unemployment rate is ignored . . . A black man in Chicago with a master's degree earns less than a white man with a high school diploma."

In a 1986 *Harper* magazine debate with conservative Charles Murray, Jackson warned against a knee-jerk negative reaction to the state and its policies to assist the poor.

"We cannot be blindly anti-government," Jackson said. "The government has made significant interventions in many, many areas for the common good. Without public schools, most Americans would not be educated. Without land-grant colleges, the United States would not have the number one agricultural system in the world. Without the federal transit programs, we would not have an interstate highway system. Without subsidized hospitals, most Americans could not afford decent medical care . . . But when we shift from the notion of subsidy as something that serves our national interest, to that of welfare, then attitudes suddenly shift from negative to positive."

As the most gifted and vigilant black leader in the post-King era, Jackson has helped to guide black America through cycles of white backlash, the assertion of black power, the institutionalization and attack on affirmative action, Reaganism, post–civil rights racial politics, the social and racial consequences of crack, the age of hip hop, and bitter black class warfare. Long before recent heated debates about black self-help and personal responsibility, Jackson argued that black parents should take an active role in their children's education, and that inner city children should attend to their school lessons, through his PUSH/Excel program. Jackson was criticized for "blaming the victim," but after conceding that blacks "are the victims and the oppressor is the victimizer," he argued that there "are just some things that people can't do for you, that you have to do for yourself. Of all of your powers—your political power, your economic power, and your social power—no power is more fundamental than willpower." Jackson said that he wanted youth to understand that they "need their willpower developed. It's bad to be in the slums, but it's even worse when the slums get in you." Jackson said, "Self-determination is our goal, and self-discipline, self-initiative, and self-awareness are necessary to get self-government." Jackson proclaimed that what "we must do today is raise the expectation levels of our people."

Jackson's two presidential races, in 1984 and 1988, altered the black political landscape. Jackson garnered 3.5 million voters in his first run for the White House, and more than doubled that number in 1988. His efforts registered massive numbers of black citizens and mobilized progressives across the country. Jackson founded the National Rainbow Coalition in 1984 to forge connections among various racial and ethnic groups with an eye to transforming the American political scene. Jackson also expanded his freedom efforts globally, winning the release of hostages and political prisoners from Kuwait to Cuba. Jackson has been a relentless force in the media, brilliantly leveraging his celebrity to explore on television and radio complex social ideas, while advocating for social change.

Jackson has largely lived up to King's beliefs that leaders be wise and in love with justice; that they be strategic in their plans to effect transformation; and that they place the interests of the folk over self-interest. To be sure, Jackson has been accused of unprincipled self-promotion, of "shaking down" corporations in the name of racial justice, of hogging the spotlight for economic benefit, and a great deal more. But King faced nearly every one of these charges from forces that sought to smear his name in bad publicity and negate the good work he did. Jackson has had to face even more criticism over the years because he lacked the benefits of martyrdom: the erasure of conflicts and contradictions and the reshaping of history to the advantage of the fallen leader. Neither did King have to deal with the sort of public embarrassment that Jackson faced when it was revealed in 2001 that he had fathered a child out of wedlock after having an extramarital affair with an aide.

Jackson's plight raises difficult questions about leadership and morality. His situation illustrates the need to acknowledge that our leaders will occasionally disappoint themselves and us. If we demand that they be perfect, we risk disillusionment when their shortcomings surface. The underlying flaw of our unwritten compact with leaders is the desperate need to believe that they must be pure to be effective. The best leaders concede their flawed humanity even as they aspire to lofty goals.

This does not mean that we should not hold leaders accountable for their actions. To his credit, Jackson acknowledged his failure, sought the forgiveness of his family and followers, and provided for his infant daughter. He is willing to practice the same moral accountability he preaches. Because Jackson has so prominently urged young people to take the high road of personal responsibility, some conclude that his actions reveal hypocrisy. But it is not hypocritical to fail to achieve the moral standards that one believes are correct. Hypocrisy comes when leaders conjure moral standards that they refuse to apply to themselves and when they do not accept the same consequences they imagine for others who offend moral standards.

We are plagued by either-or ethics. Some believe that morality is judged by examining the private behavior of leaders—that what one does in the bedroom is just as important as what one does in public. Others claim that private behavior has little consequence in measuring political character. The truth may lie somewhere between these extremes. Conservatives too often reduce the complexity of character to a test of sexual propriety. In assessing moral failure, they pay little attention to how political judgments may reveal ethical poverty. As long as a decision, say, to cut millions of the needy from welfare rolls is made by a politician without a sexual problem, the outrage it may cause is chalked up to ideology, not morality.

On the other hand, liberals are infamous for underplaying the relation between personal and public life. When liberals justly defended Bill Clinton during the impeachment debacle, few remembered that the same president had demanded Surgeon General Joycelyn Elders's resignation after she suggested that masturbation should be openly discussed with young people. The obsession with sexual sin has distorted our understanding of the morality of leadership. Our leaders cannot possibly satisfy the demand for purity that some make. And neither should they try. Leaders who are blemish-free often possess a self-satisfaction that stifles genuine leadership.

Those leaders who are in touch with their own limitations often display a political prudence that matches their personal humility. Martin Luther King, Jr.'s flaws magnify his greatness because they provide a glimpse into a soul struggling with the knowledge that he was neither perfect nor pure. King's guilt about being widely celebrated, and about his own moral failures, gave him a humility that is virtually absent in contemporary leaders. If we delude ourselves into believing that our leaders, even our heroes, have not at times fallen, we deny ourselves the powerful lessons of their struggle for moral maturity.

One of the most significant consequences of Jackson's troubles had nothing to do with his family life, but with how he became vulnerable to a challenge of his leadership of black America.

# CHAPTER
# NINE

## LAST OF A DYING BREED?

JESSE JACKSON'S DIFFICULTIES OPENED THE way for the emergence of another charismatic black leader, Al Sharpton, who looked to King and Jackson as his role models, even as he failed at times in his early career to uphold their vision for principled and careful leadership. Al Sharpton's evolution from "impulsive militant to a more responsible activist and politician" suggests that he matured when he stuck to King's and Jackson's style of leadership. Furthermore, his occasionally contentious relationship with Jackson underscores the vices of charismatic authority in black life.

The competing public images of Sharpton—glorified racial ambulance chaser, racial poseur bent on stirring controversy, camera-hogging activist more interested in the limelight than civil rights—often ignore his Pentecostal roots and the influence on his style and approach by a

diverse cadre of mentors. Sharpton, born in 1954, was
a bona fide prodigy of the black pulpit: at the age of four,
he began to extol the Lord's word in his Brooklyn Pentecostal church, and by the age of ten, the pint-sized
preacher who had been dubbed the "Wonderboy" was officially ordained. Sharpton went on preaching tours with
his Washington Temple pastor Bishop Frederick Douglas
Washington and gospel great Mahalia Jackson, for whom
Sharpton preached in 1964 in between her shows at the
New York World's Fair. Taken under wing by another
minister at his church, Sharpton read widely, learning
about Marcus Garvey and Adam Clayton Powell. During a
tour of the Caribbean, the ten-year-old minister spent a
day sipping tea with Garvey's widow, having called her on
the phone. Inspired by Powell's story, he sought out the
flamboyant congressman and pastor of Harlem's historic
Abyssinian Baptist Church. When he met him in his
study after service, Sharpton was surprised and delighted
to learn that the famed leader had already heard of him.
The two forged a relationship that influenced Sharpton's
understanding of leadership.

Sharpton turned increasingly to politics, and on a couple of occasions met Martin Luther King at Brooklyn's
branch of Operation Breadbasket, headed by Rev. William
Augustus Jones, an eloquent preacher who pastored
Bethany Baptist Church. Sharpton focused his youthful
attention elsewhere, but later, deeply affected by King's
death, he returned to Breadbasket and asked to start a

youth division. Named youth director in 1969, he met
Operation Breadbasket's national director, Jesse Jackson,
a couple of months later, and they formed a close relationship that has been sometimes sorely tested in the nearly
forty years of their association. Sharpton continued
throughout his youth to preach and engage in civil rights
protests and boycotting businesses that failed to honor
black patronage—most notably mammoth grocery chain
A&P. After graduating from high school, he became the
first person in his family to attend college, but he dropped
out of Brooklyn College after completing only two years.
Sharpton was eager to expand his leadership and, with the
aid of former King lieutenant Bayard Rustin, formed the
National Youth Movement as a vehicle for his activism.
As he raised funds for his group, Sharpton met soul
singing legend James Brown, who volunteered to help.
Brown took Sharpton on tour with him, and the two
bonded as father and son, a relationship that lasted until
Brown's death in 2006.

Sharpton's rise as a black leader in New York came at a
time when there was a displacement of manufacturing
jobs by the dominance of the financial, insurance, real
estate, and advertising sectors. As a result, the economy
shifted away from blue-collar workers and favored the
well-trained middle- and upper-managerial classes. The
New York of the seventies and eighties for black communities was marked by rising unemployment, dramatic
spikes in homelessness, and vastly increased crime driven

in large part by the crack cocaine underground economy.
Mayor Ed Koch's administration, which lasted from 1978
to 1990, was distinguished by policies and practices that
have been characterized as a war on the poor. Koch's director of human services Blanche Bernstein said that the
number of folk receiving welfare, whom Koch dubbed
"poverty pimps," would be "what she wanted it to be."
She was as good as her word: in 1978 the rejection rate for
welfare applicants nearly doubled from its 1976 level. At
the same time a zealous police state was imposed on poor
black communities, with a pronounced increase in publi-
cized police brutality cases. This is the political and social
arena into which Sharpton stepped to exercise his brand of
leadership: an aggressive public response to the erosion of
black civil rights by conjuring the parallels, and drawing
distinctions, between New York and the South; linking
his actions to, and patterning his public practice after,
that of well-known black leaders like King and Jackson,
and thus seeking to establish his pedigree and legitimacy;
and protecting the black working and working poor
classes from the invidious consequences of white hate
mobs and a vicious police state.

Sharpton's vocation as a social activist took off due to,
and was sustained by, a series of racial conflagrations in
various regions of New York, each one bringing him more
visibility and controversy in turn. In December 1984
Bernhard Geotz, the white "subway vigilante," shot four

young black men on a Manhattan subway. They had asked him for five dollars and he shot them (unloading his gun at the rate of five shots a second), he claimed, because he feared for his life. Goetz was eventually convicted of illegally possessing a weapon and spent eight months in jail, thanks in part to a series of protests that Sharpton organized. Then two years later in Howard Beach, Queens, a white Italian neighborhood, a car occupied by three black men, Cedric Sandiford, Timothy Grimes, and Michael Griffith, broke down. They looked for a phone to call for help, but facing the taunts of a group of racist whites, took refuge in a local pizzeria. When they left, the three men were harassed by the white mob, fighting with them before they fled as the crowd pursued. Sandiford and Grimes hid by an expressway, but Griffith wasn't as fortunate: he ran onto the expressway to escape and was hit by a car and killed. Sandiford said that when the police finally showed up, they treated him as the criminal, not the victim, refusing to treat his wounds and demanding to know why he'd come to Howard Beach at all. Sharpton sprang into action; his aggressive protests, including blocking the traffic on the Brooklyn Bridge and jumping onto subway tracks, and strategic advice to the victims' families, suggesting they withhold cooperation with the Queens district attorney until a special prosecutor was appointed, eventually resulted in getting the charges of "reckless endangerment" against four of the mob members upgraded to charges of murder and manslaughter. Later, three of the four men were convicted of manslaughter and with assaulting Sandiford.

Sharpton's reputation grew as he addressed every major, and minor, racial scandal in New York, especially those involving the hateful actions of white mobs or the brutality of the police. There was the 1989 case of sixteen-year-old Yusuf Hawkins, a black youth who was murdered while shopping with three other black youth for a used car in Bensonhurst, an Italian neighborhood in Brooklyn. The black men were beaten by nearly thirty white youth who had been laying in wait to exact vengeance on a black man who was dating a girl in the neighborhood. Joseph Fama was eventually sentenced to thirty-two and two-thirds years to life for shooting Hawkins twice through the heart, in part because Sharpton organized more than a score of marches to protest the injustice, bringing out the worst in Bensonhurst's white citizens, some of whom shouted "Send 'em back to Africa" and "Niggers go home." On the weekend before the King holiday in 1991, Sharpton was about to lead his twenty-ninth march in the area, when Michael Riccardi, a hateful white man, accosted him and, the portly minister thought, punched him hard in the chest. Sharpton looked down only to discover a knife handle protruding from his chest. He quickly pulled the five-inch blade out before he collapsed to his knees amidst his blood and the pandemonium of the crowd. Sharpton recovered from his attack and asked for leniency in court for his attacker, who served eight years in prison after being sentenced in 1992 to five to fifteen years on a first-degree assault conviction. After he was stabbed, Sharpton reflected on his path and formed the National Action Network to channel his social activism around voter education, poverty, and community businesses in a structured organizational environment.

But no other case got Sharpton such wide and negative notice as the Tawana Brawley case. On November 28, 1987, in the town of Wappingers Falls, New York, Brawley, a fifteen-year-old black girl, was found in a garbage bag smeared with excrement, her clothing torn and burned, with racist graffiti written on her body in charcoal. Brawley said that she had been assaulted and raped by six white men, some of them police officers. Attorneys Alton H. Maddox and C. Vernon Mason, who frequently worked with Sharpton, joined the minister in representing Brawley. A grand jury concluded after seven months of scouring police and medical records that Brawley had fabricated her story. Sharpton, Maddox, and Mason blasted back that the Dutchess County prosecutor, Steven Pagones, was a racist and accused him of being one of the perpetrators of the alleged abduction and rape. Pagones sued the controversial trio for slander and won his case. Sharpton's share in the judgment for making defamatory comments about Pagones was $65,000. Already branded a racial controversialist who provoked public spectacles to enflame, rather than dampen, the fires of racial animus,

Sharpton's reputation took a huge hit with his defense of Brawley. But it didn't keep Sharpton from being involved in other high-profile racial catastrophes, from the 1991 Crown Heights incident (a twenty-nine-year-old Jewish visiting seminary student was randomly killed in retaliation for the death earlier that day of a seven-year-old black boy who was hit as a vehicle driven by a Jewish man ran a red light); to protesting the 1999 police killing of unarmed African immigrant Amadou Diallo; spending ninety days in jail in 2001 for protesting the use of Vieques Island in Puerto Rico for bombing practice; and leading a major march in 2007 on behalf of the Jena Six in Louisiana.

Sharpton's political engagement—running for mayor of New York City, twice for the U.S. Senate, and then in 2004 for the presidency—cemented his appeal as a mainstream political force and shored up his bid to be taken seriously as a, some would argue *the*, national black leader. Sharpton's early career fell short in satisfying King's views of leadership on some accounts, especially King's insistence on planning and preparation, and in the erratic, chaotic, and anarchic elements that occasionally surrounded Sharpton's social interventions, particularly the Brawley case. Ironically, Sharpton's evolution from perceived racial hustler to respectable black leader has brought him into sharp conflict with his self-proclaimed "second hero" Jesse Jackson, a conflict that may illumine both their specific relationship and the flawed character of charismatic authority and its transmission within black leadership circles that claim King as an inspiration.

Sharpton's career has been shaped, perhaps more than most, by his models and mentors. Bishop Washington opened a window onto the Pentecostal preaching landscape for Sharpton, offering a fiery baptism into the fraternity and social rituals of livelihood made possible by plying the sacred spoken word. William August Jones gave Sharpton an appreciation for the elegant possibilities and intellectual integrity of the black sermon, and whetted Sharpton's appetite for picking up the books of the social gospel tradition in which Jones was widely read. "One of the first times I heard him speak," Sharpton recalls of Jones, "he said America was suffering from a 'faulty theology emanating from a sick sociology based in a false anthropology.'" Sharpton says that the "only other person I had ever heard with that command of the English language was Dr. King." Sharpton began to read academic theology because of Jones—everything from liberation theology, Karl Barth, Paulo Freire, Walter Rauschenbusch, as he recalls that "I'm fourteen and I'm reading this stuff because I'm around these big Baptist preachers." When Jones told him that King was deeply influenced by Rauschenbusch and the Social Gospel, Sharpton gained "even more incentive to get involved in the movement." Later, Sharpton would switch denominations from Pentecostal to Baptist, for spiritual and, arguably, political reasons.

Adam Clayton Powell gave Sharpton a sense of courageous theatricality, a flashy, stylish indifference to what
others thought as long as he wielded genuine power.
Powell's considerable self-confidence was seductive to
Sharpton, if threatening to the white world that harshly
judged him. Sharpton later came to see how Powell's out-
rageous antics worked against an appreciation for his
legitimate contributions, especially the boycotts, marches,
and sit-ins that Powell led long before his Southern peers.
"I think that the media and scholars have underplayed his
substance and real contribution," Sharpton writes. "Some
of it was Adam's fault—he was a preacher, and preachers
have a natural tendency for showmanship—but beyond
that, I think he had a very deep resentment of whites
because of how his family was treated . . ." Sharpton says
that Powell's "outrageousness was a deeply personal way of
mocking the system that had caused him such pain. And
perhaps, at times, he carried it too far, masking his own
achievement." Many critics have drawn the same conclusion about Sharpton.

James Brown was a surrogate father for Sharpton and
gave him his sense of identity as a black man. By taking
Sharpton under his wing—taking him on tour, entrusting
him with aspects of his business, showing him the personal and professional payoffs to extremely disciplined
exploitation of his talent—Brown offered Sharpton a view
of black masculinity that was responsible, hardworking,
and persevering through personal difficulty, especially

Brown's jail time and allegations of domestic violence.
Sharpton says:

> James Brown taught me more than anyone in the Civil
> Rights Movement about how to stand up, not compro-
> mise, be a man and push things as far as they can go
> . . . James took me all over the world with him . . .
> Pound for pound, he is the strongest, most courageous
> man I have ever known. Even when he was in jail, he
> didn't break, he didn't back down. There were many
> stories about him over the years of domestic violence
> and drug use, but all I can say is that I didn't see it. I
> can't say it didn't happen, but if it did, he shielded me
> from it . . . All I know is that I've learned more about
> manhood, and being a man, from him than from any-
> one else. And he's a musical genius. He can do every
> single job on one of his records, and those records are
> among the most influential in the history of popular
> music. What a man.

It was also Brown who inspired Sharpton's trademark
conked mane. Brown had been invited to the White
House in 1981 by Ronald Reagan to meet with Vice President George Bush on Martin Luther King's birthday. The
legendary entertainer insisted on bringing along his protégé Sharpton, but he first wanted him coiffed to James
Brownian perfection. "I want you to do the Reverend's
hair like mine," Brown instructed his female Georgia

hairdresser, "because when we go to the White House there's going to be a lot of press, and when people see him I want them to see me, like he's my son." As the hairdresser relaxed and rolled Sharpton's Afro, Brown extracted a pledge from him of lifelong follicle fidelity. "Reverend, I want you to make me one promise. I want you to wear your hair like that until I die." Sharpton agreed, even as he later acknowledged the alleged racial self-injury that was pressed into his curls. "People often say that wearing a process indicates self-hatred and imitates white people, but my hair has nothing to do with that; it is symbolic of my bond, very deep and intensely personal, with James Brown."

Sharpton's hair has often been, if not quite a floating signifier, then at least a bouncing metaphor, driving the black bourgeoisie mad with embarrassment that a major black leader propped up by the press is literally propped up by a press and curl. But what his black elite critics often railed against in dissing Sharpton was the working-class symbolism of the jogging suits he often sported in addition to the conk which, in an earlier generation of working-class black men known as zoot suiters, "was a refusal to look like either the dominant stereotyped image of the Southern migrant or the black bourgeoisie, whose 'conks' were closer to mimicking white styles than those of the zoot suiters." When Sharpton later ran for the White House, one couldn't help but observe the ironies of style that joined him by his hair to the presidential pedigree: anyone viewing a silhouette of George Washington juxtaposed to Al Sharpton might be hard pressed to tell the difference between the two.

But Sharpton's bread and butter—brilliantly turning the sacred spoken word to political use, using a sharp wit to underscore social suffering, dramatizing social injustice through bold public gestures, and projecting black leadership through an ethic of swagger—owes perhaps the greatest debt to his apprenticeship, and his aggravations, with Jesse Jackson. Like Jackson, Sharpton had a painful and complicated relationship with his father, who left the family home when it was discovered he had been carrying on an illicit affair with his wife's daughter from a first marriage. Eventually they had a son, who was both Sharpton's brother and nephew. Those events not only traumatized the nine-year-old preacher, but thrust Sharpton and his mother and other sister from a comfortable existence into poverty and the projects. Like Jackson, Sharpton was influenced by King, though he obviously didn't enjoy the close bond between Jackson and King. Sharpton was deeply affected by King's death. "I was sad," he writes. "I worked in his Breadbasket program and was a youth minister. I met Dr. King a couple of times. He knew me as 'the boy preacher.' When he would see me, he would say, 'There goes that boy preacher!' and a big grin would break over his face. I felt good being a part of something he was involved in, and the loss was definitely felt." But it wasn't until a year later when he viewed the theatrical release of the poignant documentary *King: From Montgomery to Memphis* that he fully felt the impact of King's death, moving him to shape his life around the themes of King's career. "That's when it hit me," Sharpton says. "All those things he did, all those freedoms he fought for, all those laws that got overturned to make life better for all people—what would happen now?" Sharpton made up his mind to work in Operation Breadbasket "to carry on Dr. King's legacy."

Jackson was the most direct link to King's legacy, and a crucial influence on Sharpton's view and style of leadership. Sharpton says that "Jesse Jackson is probably the smartest person I know. There's no one I know who has a more brilliant, fertile mind. He is hardworking. I learned about the value of getting up early every morning from Jesse. And he is very, very committed." Sharpton says he had read about Jackson "in magazines and seen him on television, and I liked his style. He was young, brash, had a huge Afro, and wore a medallion. I started wearing a medallion to emulate him." When Jackson came to town a couple months after Sharpton had been named youth director of Operation Breadbasket, the fourteen-year-old preacher got pithy, direct advice from his hero, who, according to Sharpton, didn't look at him but rather past him. "All you got to do is choose your targets and kick ass." Later, when Jackson's friend, and Sharpton's sometime touring mate, Mahalia Jackson arrived and showed the young preacher love, it broke the ice between him and his soon to be idol. From that night on, Jackson and Sharpton "became tight."

When he saw Jackson reading Paul Tillich's *Love, Power and Justice,* he went out and purchased and read Tillich's corpus. Sharpton was "imitating my mentor, but also expanding myself as a person," saying that it's very "important whom you choose as your mentor" because "their heroes become your heroes, their ideological bent becomes of serious interest to you." When Sharpton dropped out of college—a decision he later regretted, but which at the time made sense to him because he knew "all these heavy hitters" so "what do I need a degree for?"— Jackson mercilessly teased and shamed him in the acerbic way that those in Jackson's orbit sometimes feel. "Here come the boy wonder, ain't gonna be nothing but a Harlem fanatic," Jackson sarcastically offered. Sharpton resented it, but he came to see that Jackson understood that he needed serious preparation for the long haul. "I thought he was trying to stifle me, that all the people applauding were the ones who cared. But it was the opposite, wasn't it? He never gave me undue credit; with him I had to earn everything twice, which is what any young person needs."

After Sharpton became a figure in his own right, Jackson offered him advice on how to handle stinging criticism as they listened to a radio talk show guest run Sharpton down. "Before you even say anything about this, let me tell you something," Jackson instructed Sharpton. "This used to happen to me in Chicago all the time. But have you ever been in a football game? If you've played football, you noticed that the players, the offense and the defense, they're all thinking about one thing. The guy with the ball. If everybody's after you, it must be that you have the ball. Nobody's chasing anybody that doesn't have the ball." Sharpton derived consolation from Jackson's story and concluded that if "I'm the one they all want to tackle, it's because they're afraid that I may score." Jackson also helped Sharpton understand the difference between good and great leaders. "Good leaders are famous, energizing types of people, inspirational to all kinds of people," Jackson told Sharpton. "But great leaders are those who can learn to suffer and take pain, and still give out positive auras and inspirational hope while never betraying the pain they experienced. That's what made Dr. King great, what made Nelson Mandela great." Sharpton drew from Jackson's words the lesson that "pain is part of the price you pay if you're going to lead, and if you're not willing to pay that price, you ought not to lead."

Sharpton claims he and Jackson had their first trouble when Jackson insisted that Sharpton's relationship with James Brown would distract him from his civil rights work. Sharpton believed that Jackson was jealous of his close relationship to the entertainer, and besides, Jackson maintained friendships with Hollywood celebrities, so his association with Brown should be no bother. But in the late 1980s, Sharpton says the two grew apart because of Sharpton's ties to black nationalists, who proved strong critics of Jackson's integrationist politics. They continued to drift apart until Sharpton was stabbed in 1991, when he and Jackson reconciled and talked every day, sometimes two and three times a day, for the next seven years. But in the late 1990s, he and Jackson suffered strained relations as Sharpton questioned the direction of Jackson's commitment to civil rights as he became close to Bill Clinton. "I felt his relationship with Clinton and the White House was getting in the way of his work as an activist," Sharpton says. "I felt that if he was going to represent the civil rights cause, the human rights cause, Jesse had to choose between whether he was going to be part of the structure or challenge the structure." Then, turning King's example on Jackson, Sharpton argues that "Dr. King, as close as he was to Lyndon Johnson, came out vocally against the war in Vietnam. He never took a presidential appointment. He challenged the system."

Sharpton says that he had "tactical discomfort" with Jackson's confusing inside-outside strategy—"You need both, but you can't be both"—in his relations to Wall Street and the White House. "While Jesse was inside the White House with Clinton, I was outside calling for economic accountability on Wall Street. I was outside, calling Clinton's hand on welfare reform and the onerous crime bill. Jesse was virtually silent on those issues. He was an insider. And after seven years of us being close again, we started to split." Their split was exacerbated when, Sharpton says, Jackson publicly disagreed with Sharpton's boycott of Burger King. Sharpton couldn't "believe that he, who taught me in my youth about fighting these corporations and making them accountable, would publicly come out against my doing the very thing he taught me to do." Sharpton took comfort in history, noting that Jackson didn't receive the support of Andrew Young and Coretta Scott King when he ran for president, wondering if he was going through with Jackson what he went through with them. "But I would have thought that he might not want to do that to the next generation."

Sharpton's claim that "[c]ontrary to popular belief, we didn't split over his scandal with Karin Stanford and the baby he had out of wedlock," but over philosophy, has been challenged by a damning December 2004 story in the *Village Voice* that persuasively argues that Sharpton "helped engineer the demise of his mentor, Jesse Jackson, who had an affair with the executive director of his nonprofit organization and showered her with benefits, even while Sharpton was sending every signal to those around him that he was doing the same." According to the *Voice*, four top Sharpton associates "participated in a news barrage against Jesse Jackson early in 2001 that elevated Sharpton to a new national status," or as a related *Voice* article said, that "catapulted Sharpton to the top ranks of African American leadership." One of those associates, Harold Doley Jr.—the first black to win a seat on the

New York Stock Exchange and a key figure in Jackson's Wall Street Project, and as a black Republican millionaire, a Sharpton financial supporter—suggesting that Sharpton may have done precisely what he claimed Jackson did by confusing the inside-outside on Wall Street, told the *Voice*: "I said to Sharpton, 'I'm going to bring Jesse down and make you the man.' Al said, 'I'm ready.'" And if the charges are true that Sharpton was carrying on an affair with his then chief of staff, even as Jackson was being pilloried in the press at his bidding, then his claims to the *Nation* in April 2001 (when he was allegedly in the thick of the tryst) that he "got that impulse [to cheat] out my system when I was on the road with James Brown all those years" rings especially false and hypocritical.

Sharpton may have a legitimate beef with Jackson over differing philosophies and conflicting approaches to protests and the ethics of black leadership. But if true, his alleged takedown of his mentor so that he might ascend to his throne burns with Shakespearean tragedy. It also underscores some of the vulnerabilities and weaknesses of charismatic authority: it hinges on displacement and deceit, on vanity and viciousness, on the part of those who would carve their niche on the totem pole of black leadership. It also highlights the rule of ruthless ambition in charismatic leadership circles where the desire to point the way and be on top is a classic example of King's warning against the "drum major instinct." Instead of seeking to serve, the desire for premier status, to serve as "president

of black America" among charismatic black leaders, fosters
an intensely competitive, and often lethal, environment
fueled by *succession syndrome.*

In Jackson's case, whatever one may conclude about the
fatal ambition that drove him to become King's replace-
ment before the leader was even laid to rest, at least King
was dead, and equally important, Jackson hadn't killed
him off, either literally or symbolically. But in Sharpton's
seizure of uncontrollable ambition, lacking the convenience of a brilliantly dead mentor whom he might praise
and replace, he contrived to knock Jackson off by slicing a
symbolic jugular, the vitally important vein of his public
reputation. By doing his mentor in and offering himself
up as Jackson's defender and successor, Sharpton unwittingly revealed the poisonous sentiments on which charismatic leadership and succession syndrome depend.

It may be a bitter irony as well that Sharpton's recent
campaign against the lethal intensities of hip hop—its
murderous misogyny and epithet-laden rage—have nothing on the internecine injuries that black leaders impose
on one another when they want to be the H.N.I.C. Charismatic black figures say "nigga" must be shed from the
linguistic arsenal of the young, but it has hardly been dis-
placed, at least in one of its negative incarnations, as the
spiritual basis of intramural contests among black male
leaders. Sharpton is a man of enormous gifts, a former
wunderkind of black homiletics who fulfilled his early
promise with a biting, brilliant tongue in defense of the

vulnerable, and with a skilled and inventive leadership
that, at its best, extends the legacy of King and Jackson.
He is the last member of a genre and style of leadership
that is quickly passing off the scene, forced away as much
by new conditions of culture as by the increased options
available to a risen black middle class. But the persistent
poverty of struggling blacks, and newfangled forms of
racism, mean that another charismatic black leader in
the mode of King, Jackson, and Sharpton may always be
needed. Sharpton has also consciously, and in masterly
fashion, rehabilitated his image from that of an itinerant
race hustler to a respected national black leader. If Jackson
has begrudged or blocked his ascent, it is a severe mark
against his noble and legendary leadership. But if the allegations of Sharpton's betrayal of Jackson are true, the
unconscionable means elected to achieve his position are a
blight on his record and that of charismatic black leadership. Perhaps another example of leadership, one rooted in
political and institutional authority, offers a fresh vision of
how charismatic authority can be channeled into social
good for black America, and help to fulfill King's vision
of redemptive black political leadership.

# CHAPTER
# TEN

# BLACK KENNEDY

THE RISE OF BARACK OBAMA AS THE MOST
popular and potentially powerful black American politician ever is at once a nod to King's legacy and a pioneering venture into new territory. Obama's historic quest for
the presidency—winning more than twenty-five primaries
and caucuses both in predominantly black states and in
states with overwhelming white populations—has also
revealed the complicated politics of race for the Joshuas
who seek to blaze a path toward the Promised Land.

Obama is, no doubt, the product of a paradox: he rests
atop an inverted racial pyramid that he has been credited
with overturning, and yet without the fierce rumblings of
race that his ascent seems to overcome, his career, and now
his campaign for the presidency, wouldn't necessarily be
seen as the miracle of transcendence for which they've
been touted. Obama's promise as a black man who bears

none of the scorn or rancor of his civil rights predecessors is a double-edged razor: one of the reasons he's able to be the man he is—to have the noble bearing of a statesman who wants to get past the arguments of the past—is because those arguments were made, and bitter battles were fought, and in some cases are still being fought. But the division of labor throws many people off: it appears that the either-or thinking that Obama wants to sail beyond has trapped those who applaud his success. If Barack Obama now, or some black person in the future, should become president, neither Jesse Jackson nor Al Sharpton would be out of a job. A black president can't end black misery; a black president can't be a civil rights leader or primarily a crusader for racial justice. A black president won't stop racism or erase bigotry. A black president won't be the president of blacks alone, but the president of the United States. That tricky but not trivial difference suggests that prophets of the people won't go unemployed when politicians of the race do well. In fact, quite the opposite is true.

Obama himself recognized this difference when he answered a question put to him and his peers by journalist Wolf Blitzer during a debate for Democratic presidential candidates in South Carolina on the 2008 King Holiday. "If Dr. Martin Luther King were alive today, why should he endorse you?" "Well, I don't think Dr. King would endorse any of us," Obama responded. "I think what he would call upon the American people to do is to hold us accountable . . . I believe change does not happen from the top down; it happens from the bottom up. Dr. King understood that. It was those women who were willing to walk instead of ride the bus. [It was] union workers who were willing to take on violence and intimidation to get the right to organize. It was women who decided, 'You know, I'm as smart as my husband; I'd better get the right to vote.' Them arguing, mobilizing, agitating and ultimately *forcing* elected officials to be accountable. I think that's the key." Jesse Jackson and Al Sharpton and a legion of activists are the arguers, mobilizers, and agitators who force the Barack Obamas and other elected officials to be accountable.

This doesn't mean that Obama lacks the urgent sense of destiny that only a few politicians have ever truly possessed in American life. This is not to be confused with the gutless swagger of the younger Bush's revamped Manifest Destiny, or the perilous and bloated delusions of Richard Nixon. Ever since he roared into our ears in eloquent cadence at the podium of the 2004 Democratic National Convention, Barack Obama has struck new chords in American politics. He has made millions believe that their elected leaders might dare to dream out loud and not mind saying so. He makes one feel that he can cast aside rigid categories and rise above the plodding aspirations that weigh down too many politicians. His written word sings; his spoken word soars on the wings of renewed faith in the democratic process, and how we need such renewal in an ugly age of despotic indifference to the freedom to think creatively. Obama's eyes are fixed on what we can make together of our national future.

To see what makes Obama tick, look at his training in the trenches of community organizing. As Ronald Reagan practiced what Vice President George Bush would call "voodoo economics"—supply-side theories wrapped in tax cuts for the wealthy—Obama exited the Ivy League corridors of Columbia University in 1983. After a brief and unsatisfying stint on Wall Street, he headed straight for the 'hood. On the South Side of Chicago, he worked with a church-based group that battled poverty's offspring: crime and high unemployment. Obama rolled up his sleeves—something he got used to doing to satisfy his basketball jones on countless asphalt courts—and applied elbow grease and hard thinking to the persistent ills of the poor. Practical efforts to help the beleaguered are good training for leaders of the free world. The poignant memory of the most afflicted stands a better chance to replay in their minds.

Young Obama soon learned the limits of local remedies. Soon he imagined how law and politics might help him change lives at the national level. This was at a time when Reagan feasted on skepticism about government to help ordinary people. Obama's hopeful—but far from naive—belief in the political process sent him to Harvard Law School in the late eighties. He kept in hand a round-trip ticket back to Chicago, where he served as an Illinois state senator for eight years before entering the U.S. Senate in 2004. Obama's community organizing and work in the Illinois Senate offer a glimpse of his political pedigree—especially his bipartisan efforts to earn families across the state more than $100 million in tax cuts, his advocacy of legislation in support of early childhood education, and his opposition to racial profiling. But so does his brief stay in the U.S. Senate. Obama has fought for disability pay for veterans. He has worked to boost the nonproliferation of deadly weapons. He has advocated the use of alternative fuels to cure our national addiction to oil. He has scolded the Bush administration for its vicious indifference to the poor, and for its political incompetence in the wake of Hurricane Katrina. He has rallied as well against genocide in Darfur. Long before it was popular, he stood against the war in Iraq. He saw early that it was a futile gesture of American empire that would do little to beat back the threat of terror. Sadly, his prophesy has been confirmed in the numbers of dead and the relentless pace of destruction.

It is one thing to say that Obama's credentials for public service have been gained in the give-and-take of community organizing and power politics. But his belief in the American people is a reflection, in part, of the profound belief they have invested in him. His belief also greatly borrows from his trafficking in the cross-sections of various cultures, colors, and communities. Obama's roots in more than one race, and his experiences in many cultures, are not, as falsely advertised, a liability. But there has been a great deal of Obamanxiety; in fact, there's been a war in Barack, that is, in his metaphoric body, which captures the insular and insidious nature of so much talk about blackness and race. The debate about whether or not Obama is black enough rests on a bad misreading of the politics of race in black America. That debate has jumped off more in media than in the mouths of everyday black folk longing to know more about Obama's politics, not his pigment.

Before he rose to fame, there was little doubt that Obama was black. He moved to the South Side of Chicago, home to black communities that have spawned sociological classics by Cayton and Drake and William Julius Wilson. He took a low-paying job to work largely among the black poor. He joined the blackest church in town, for which he's taken considerable heat from the right-wing media. He twice ran and lost a bid for Congress against an icon of sixties black struggle. He married a brilliant and beautiful and unmistakably black woman—for all, and for what, that's worth—with whom he is rearing two bright and lovely black daughters. But there's an understandable phenomenon that happens in black life—though, to tell the truth, it is sometimes completely befuddling when it gets evoked. It issues in an informal axiom: when white folk like a black person too much, there's usually something really wrong with them. Or, in its worse incarnation, they must be really bad for

228

black folk: either they hate us because they hate themselves, or they despise our pride in them and covet the
alienated status that they wear as a badge in white America. The latter usually happens among blacks seeking the
approval of the far right, and the former among a small
percentage of blacks who, because they were reared in
largely white areas around white folk, simply can't imagine why they must wear the skin of the people most foreign to them.

But that litmus test doesn't always work; Martin
Luther King fought the perception that he was an Uncle
Tom or a sellout among some black factions because he
moved effortlessly between white and black America.
Neither can it entirely predict how black folk will behave
toward a black refugee who is forced out of seclusion in
largely white enclaves. O. J. Simpson was never seen
before he was accused of murder as a black man by most
black folk; but when he fell so far so fast—and when *Time*
magazine blackened his face like a meal of catfish on its
cover—O.J. was received back into black arms and hearts.
It is supremely ironic, perhaps even tragic, that a man like
Simpson, accused of murder with an extraordinary amount
of evidence amassed against him, could receive the black
benefit of doubt, and yet in some quarters, Obama
couldn't pass the smell test.

Blackness, incidentally, has never really been about
genetics anyway. That's because most black folk could
point to somebody in their family tree who couldn't pass

muster as pure Nubian ancestry. The varied skin shades testified to broad patterns of racial mixing that black folk took for granted. And trying to reduce race——any race, but especially blackness——to a genetic calculation is nearly beside the point. What disturbs or assures us about race has very little to do with blood or biology. Sure, your color can get you pulled over for driving your Ferrari in a white neighborhood, and it can get you followed in a store where they think you don't have enough plastic to ring the cash register. But race plays out in the streets and in our culture in a far more complicated way. Its about how you use language, understand your heritage, interpret your history, identify with your kin, and figure out your meaning and worth to a society that places values on you beyond your control.

And it's also about what people see you as——or take you to be. You might protest, for example, to a passing cabbie that you are a mixture of many races, and he might keep going because you look like you're black. But the cue he gets from your color isn't about your pigment alone; it's about what that color means to him, how it's been jammed into his mind with a slew of stereotypes about what a person who looks like you is likely to do, namely rob, cheat, or kill him. He didn't get that from a DNA swab; he got that from talking heads on television seeking to warn him about the carnage you might inflict——or, perhaps, from the latest 50 Cent video. All of this makes it awfully futile to string Obama up on a genetic tree and hang him for not being black enough, because, in the mother of all ironies, his mother is white and his father is African. The black folk claiming that he's not black the way they want him to be black—that he wasn't born of an American black father and mother—are pretty humorless and miss the irony of claiming that a black man born of immediate African ancestry doesn't measure up to their test of blackness.

Black folk have every right to ask if Obama will betray them, to see if he is more Clarence Thomas than Martin Luther King. And they have a right to be nervous about all the talk about post-racial identity, knowing full well that such a possibility is not only relatively slim, but that it's not a norm that should even be embraced. One need not stop being black in order to be a full citizen of the nation. Bland racial identities are not required to help the nation to a fair and just polity. We should not be post-racial: seeking to get beyond the uplifting meanings and edifying registers of blackness. Rather, we should be post-racist: moving beyond cultural fascism and vicious narratives of racial privilege and superiority that tear at the fabric of "e pluribus unum."

The challenge to black folk is to see that at least three different strategies of black identity are constantly in play to manage our lives on a cosmic level. These strategies offer the world a picture of how we understand our blackness. The first strategy is *accidental blackness:* we, by the accident of birth, simply happen to be black. In this strategy, our blackness is only the most obvious, not the most important, element of our identity. The second strategy of blackness is *incidental blackness:* we are proud to be black, but it is but one strand of our identity. Our blackness is surely important and valued, but it is not the only feature of our identity that occupies our minds. Finally, there is *intentional blackness:* we are proud of our blackness and see it as a vital, though not the exclusive, aspect of our identity. Our blackness is understood in its political forms and its social manifestations. These strategies permit black folk to operate in the world with a bit of sanity and grace. Black folk pass in and out of these strategies over a lifetime. And one can be intentionally black in one setting—say in a protest march against police brutality—and incidentally black at the company picnic. Circumstances and politics make all the difference in how and when these strategies of blackness play out.

These strategies must be kept in mind when assessing a figure like Obama. Like all black folk, he may deploy a variety of blackness depending on where he is and to whom he is speaking. When Obama was speaking before a black crowd in South Carolina during his campaign there, he used words and ideas sure to connect with them on a visceral, cultural, and racial level: he talked about being "hoodwinked" and "bamboozled" by misleading characterizations of his ideas, clearly signifying on Malcolm X's use of those terms. Obama was clearly being intentionally black. When Obama speaks before a diverse crowd of folk, he may include concerns about racial profiling with the need to clean up the environment; he's being incidentally black in such a setting. And where Obama means to unite the nation by referring to the grand ideals of the Constitution, suggesting that all Americans must forge unity around common hopes for future prosperity, he is being accidentally black. The circumstances and political objectives determine what strategies of blackness are most salient and purposeful. It is quite legitimate to question whether the use of particular strategies of blackness will work against a just polity for black folk. Still, we must be conscious that varying, sometimes even competing, strategies are at work.

This is especially true in light of the contentious racial politics of the 2008 presidential campaign. Former president Bill Clinton, a vigorous surrogate for his wife, presidential candidate Senator Hillary Clinton, caused a stir when he stated on the *Charlie Rose* show that voters who chose to support someone of Obama's experience were willing to "roll the dice" with the presidency. Some critics thought that Clinton's comment, whether intentional or not, was a subtle racial reference to urban black manhood dressed in full dice-throwing stereotypical garb. Obama, however, stayed above the fray and simply gave Clinton a taste of his own medicine, quoting the former president when he was similarly berated for a lack of experience during his 1992 run for the Oval Office: "The same old experience is irrelevant. You can have the right kind of experience or the wrong kind of experience. And mine is rooted in the real lives of real people, and it will bring real results if we have the courage to change."

Clinton also accused the press of being blinkered by Obama's charisma and not challenging his contention that he was the only Democratic presidential candidate to consistently oppose the war in Iraq. Clinton argued that while Obama stood against the war before joining the Senate, he made a statement in 2004 that he couldn't say how he would have voted on the war had he been in the Senate. Thus, Clinton concluded, his consistent antiwar claim was a fabrication. "This thing is the biggest fairy tale I've ever seen." Again, critics charged Clinton with subtle racial hints that Obama as a black man wasn't a substantial and serious candidate, though Clinton insisted on Al Sharpton's radio show that he was only referring to Obama's record, not his candidacy. Obama accused Clinton of distorting his statement, noting that the former president failed to cite his closing caveat: that from where he stood, the case hadn't been made.

Again Obama refused to bite the race apple. But facing the prospect of race-baiting in his South Carolina homestead where a major primary was approaching, and in a state where half the Democratic voters were black, James Clyburn, the highest-ranking black in Congress, expressed disappointment and called on Clinton to tone things down and "chill." Clyburn insisted that Clinton couldn't campaign for his wife in a way that would "engender the kind of feelings that seem to be bubbling up as a result of this . . . He is revered in many sections of the African-American community, and I think he can afford to tone it down."

Neither was Clyburn pleased with Hillary Clinton's comments to the Fox News Chanel suggesting that President Lyndon Johnson was more critical than Martin Luther King in getting the Civil Rights Act made into law. Clinton said that "I would point to the fact that Dr. King's dream began to be realized when President Johnson passed the Civil Rights Act of 1964, when he was able to get through Congress something that President Kennedy was hopeful to do, the president before had not even tried, but it took a president to get it done. That dream became a reality, the power of that dream became real in people's lives because we had a president who said we're going to do it, and actually got it accomplished." Clinton's comments were meant to counter Obama's frequent references to King and to assert the importance of presidential leadership. House majority whip Clyburn said in the *New York Times:* "We have to be very, very careful about how we speak about that era in American politics. It is one thing to run a campaign and be respectful of everyone's motives and actions, and it is something else to denigrate those. That bothered me a great deal."

Obama had refrained from speaking about race in the campaign, but he couldn't resist commenting on Clinton's remarks. "Senator Clinton made an unfortunate remark, an ill-advised remark, about King and I didn't make the statement. I haven't remarked on it. And she, I think, offended some folks who felt that somehow diminished King's role in bringing about the Civil Rights Act. She is free to explain that. But the notion that somehow this is our doing is ludicrous."

Bill Clinton threw even more fuel on the racial flame when he downplayed Obama's huge victory in the South Carolina primary and suggested it was a result of the state's black population and Obama's large black following. "Jesse Jackson won South Carolina in '84 and '88. Jackson ran a good campaign. And Obama ran a good campaign here." Many black folk took the equation of Jackson and Obama as a not-so-subtle attempt to ghetto-ize Obama as a "black" candidate and undercut his trans-racial appeal.

*New York Times* columnist Frank Rich argues that such racial politics are a central feature of the Clinton camp's efforts to defeat Obama.

The campaign's other most potent form of currency remains its thick deck of race cards . . . In October [2007], seven months after the two candidates' dueling church perorations in Selma, *USA Today* found Hillary Clinton leading Mr. Obama among African-American Democrats by a margin of 62 percent to 34 percent. But once black voters met Mr. Obama and started to gravitate toward him, Bill Clinton and the campaign's other surrogates stopped caring about what African-Americans thought. In an effort to scare off white voters, Mr. Obama was ghettoized as a cocaine user (by the chief Clinton strategist, Mark Penn, among others), "the black candidate" (as Clinton strategists told the Associated Press) and Jesse Jackson redux (by Mr. Clinton himself) . . . Meanwhile, the Clinton campaign's attempt to drive white voters away from Mr. Obama by playing the race card has backfired. His white vote tally rises every week. Though Mrs. Clinton won California by almost 10 percentage points, among whites she beat Mr. Obama by only 3 points.

With the exception of the dustup over Clinton's comments on Martin Luther King and Lyndon Baines Johnson, Obama has steadfastly resolved to steer his campaign away from the orbit of race. As a candidate for the presidency who happens to be black—and here Obama's accidental blackness is a vital means to assure his appeal to *all* Americans—taking the racial high road is both intrinsically rewarding and strategically necessary. If Obama is successfully painted into a racial corner as "the black candidate," he not only loses his effectiveness as a viable contender in the mainstream, but he compromises the ability to uplift black constituents. If Obama can't get elected to help *all* Americans—and while black Americans are key to his election, blacks alone can't elect him—he can't get elected to help *any* Americans, including black Americans.

Obama must sort through three models of leadership in dealing with the issue of race. The first model of leadership is one that *transcends* race. In one version of race transcending leadership, key features of the racial situation are suppressed. The nation's racial past is largely ignored. Any race conscious social remedies or political prescriptions are strictly forbidden and negatively viewed. Although this option is seductive, it is ultimately one that will not serve Obama or the nation well. Such an approach is based on a willful amnesia about race that is too steep a price to pay in order to reach what is essentially a false racial peace, an empty racial accord.

The second model is one that *translates* race. In this model of leadership, all the significant features of the social order are spoken in the language of race, are translated into the idiom of color. In this model, all social forms and facts only make sense when they refer to race. For instance, the problems of gender and class are denied the right to sit on their own analytical bottoms, or to occupy their own theoretical space. This model is too narrow because it reduces the complex social strata to its racial dimensions, while other compelling features of the social order are slighted, ignored, or erased. This model compensates the failure to consider race with the equally flawed approach of only considering race.

Finally, there is leadership that *transforms* race. In this model, a compelling account of racial facts and history is joined to an articulation of what race can and should be.

This model offers Obama the greatest intellectual and political freedom to explore the history of race while transforming its meaning in the future. Race transforming leadership does three good things: acknowledges racial facts and history, challenges racial orthodoxies, and links anti-racist struggle to other forms of political struggle. Acknowledging the history of racial suffering and strife in America is a vital necessity for all American politicians, including Obama. It assures sufficient recognition of the bitter struggles to overcome bigotry and to undo centuries of structural oppression.

But there is a need as well to challenge racial orthodoxies. For instance, the reluctance of the liberals and the left to speak forthrightly about issues of value and virtue must be criticized. Just because the right gets it wrong doesn't mean that the left should overlook the role of moral and spiritual values in the social reconstruction of black America. We have ceded this territory for far too long to conservative interests that exploit narrow views of black morality, especially in the attack on sexual minorities and the young. On the other hand, race-transforming leaders must cry out against vicious political attacks on poor black communities and the resources needed to strengthen their social standing.

Finally, race-transforming leaders must accent the centrality of race while denying the exclusivity of race. The long and bitter history of race means that its effect on American life should never be underplayed or ignored.

But it must also be acknowledged that even issues of race are shaped by factors like gender, class, sexuality, region, and religion. Forging coalitions is critical to the political behavior of race-transforming leaders, playing to Obama's strengths. In fact, Obama's racial experiences may offer him an edge in the national effort to overcome the poisonous divisions that plague the American soul. His fascinating mix of race and culture shows up in lively fashion— including his love for the upper reaches of Abraham Lincoln's emancipating political vision, as well as his compassion for the black boys and girls stuck on the lowest rung of the ladder of upward mobility. That he is aware of race without being its prisoner—that he is rooted in, but not restricted by, his blackness—challenges orthodoxies and playbooks on all sides of the racial divide. But it may also make him curiously effective in the pledge to overcome our racial malaise and to restore our national kinship.

Barack Obama has come closer than any figure in recent history to obeying a direct call of the people to the brutal and bloody fields of political mission. His visionary response to that call gives great hope that he can galvanize our nation with the payoff of his political rhetoric: a true democracy fed by justice, one that balances liberty with responsibility. He may be our best hope to tie together the fraying strands of our political will into a powerful and productive vision of national destiny, one for which Mar-

tin Luther King, Jr., hoped and died. If King was Moses
who couldn't get to the Promised Land with us, then
Jackson, Sharpton, and Obama—and Susan Taylor, Max-
ine Waters, Carolyn Cheek Kilpatrick, Marian Wright
Edelman, and many, many more—may be the Joshuas to
take us further still. Obama recognized the legacy of the
Joshua generation, and exhorted it to fulfill its obligation
to lead in a speech at Howard University's convocation,
words that are fit for us all.

> Most of you know that Moses was called by God to
> lead his people to the Promised Land. And in the face
> of a Pharaoh and his armies, across an unforgiving
> desert and along the walls of an angry sea, he succeeded
> in leading his people out of bondage in Egypt. He led
> them through great dangers, and they got far enough
> so that Moses could point the way towards freedom on
> the far banks of the river Jordan.
>
> And yet, it was not in God's plan to have Moses
> cross the river. Instead He would call on Joshua to fin-
> ish the work that Moses began. He would ask Joshua
> to take his people that final distance.
>
> Everyone in this room stands on the shoulders of
> many Moses. They are the courageous men and women
> who marched and fought and bled for the rights and
> freedoms we enjoy today. They have taken us many
> miles over an impossible journey.

But you are members of the Joshua Generation. And it is now up to you to finish the work that they began. It is up to you to cross the river.

When Joshua discovered the challenge he faced, he had his doubts and his worries. But the Lord told Joshua not to fear. He said, "Be strong and have courage, for I am with you wherever you go."

Those are the words I will leave you with today. Be strong and have courage. Be strong and have courage in the face of injustice. Be strong and have courage in the face of prejudice and hatred. Be strong and have courage in the face of joblessness and helplessness and hopelessness. Be strong and have courage, in the face of our doubts and fears, in the face of skepticism, in the face of cynicism, in the face of a mighty river. Be strong and have courage and let us cross over to that Promised Land together.

Perhaps even more than Joshua, Obama is like his biblical namesake Barak, who is described in the New Testament (along with other judges) as one "who through faith conquered kingdoms, administered justice, and gained what was promised." Obama has a real chance to embody the stable, principled black political leadership that King envisioned. And by administering justice and gaining what has been promised, Obama has an authentic opportunity to fulfill the legacy of King, and of Jesse Jackson too. Because King and Jackson fought bitter battles with ugly forces, Obama can gracefully walk through doors kicked in by King and Jackson. As he walks through those doors, Obama carries the legacy of his people even as he seeks to serve the entire nation. There could hardly be a more fitting tribute to King, and to the people and justice he loved.

# AFTERWORD

## Interview with Dr. King on His 80th Birthday

If Dr. King had lived, what might he say about what he sees today? This is but a small piece of what I think he might have thought about a few personal and social issues, offered in the same spirit that he penned his letter to the American church as the Apostle Paul. The occasion for the interview is a celebration of Dr. King's 80th birthday, which, of course, had he lived, would be nowhere near a national holiday.

QUESTION: Dr. King, how does it feel to turn 80 years old? It's such a milestone.

DR. MARTIN LUTHER KING: I must confess to you that I never thought I'd make it to this age. During the most intense moments of our struggle, there was a great deal of hatred and danger directed at us. I personally faced constant death threats. Many of our greatest leaders and most stalwart activists were brutally murdered. Medgar Evers was shot down like an animal in Mississippi, and in the same state, those three brave young civil rights workers were viciously murdered. And one can't forget the incredible sacrifice that those four young girls made when they were blown to premature martyrdom in the 16th Street Baptist Church bombing in Birmingham, Alabama. Spike Lee's very fine documentary, *Four Little Girls,* captures the sense of terror we all faced during those times, but also the dignity and courage of the people too.

As far back as 1956 I had to face the real possibility that I would die. After all, my house was bombed during the Montgomery bus boycott. When I look back on many of the sermons and speeches that I gave during the sixties, I can clearly see that I was trying to address our people's grief and suffering, and trying to inspire them to keep going in the midst of the death and hatred we faced on a daily basis. But to be honest, I was also trying to come to grips with my own mortality in a movement where it seemed guaranteed that I would be made a sacrificial lamb. But contrary to what some might have believed, I had no martyr complex. I repeatedly stated that I wanted to live as long as anybody, and so . . .

QUESTION: Well, that's certainly borne out by a statement you made in Montgomery, Alabama, in May of 1965, where you expressed a great deal of frustration and anger over the killing of Negroes while the government sat idly by. You said that "when they kill Negroes and civil rights workers in Alabama, nothing is done about it. Under the administration of Governor George Wallace alone 10 people have been killed during civil rights demonstrations." Do you remember that statement?

KING: Absolutely, like it was yesterday. I also said, "What we are saying now is that we are tired of this. Our lives are too precious. We are saying to the State of Alabama, now you're not going to frighten us into submission. If you kill one Negro, or one white ally, then you're going to have to kill ten, and if you kill ten, you're going to have to kill 20, and if you kill 20, you're going to have to kill 100, and if you kill 100, then you're going to have to kill a thousand!"

QUESTION: But did you ever have a stronger sense you were going to die than at other times? There's famous newsreel footage of you explaining in rather stark and dramatic terms how you thought you were going to die one night in Philadelphia, Mississippi. Could that be considered such a moment?

KING: Yes, it really can. There were policemen who were preceding us as we marched, and they spotted several people in trees ahead of us, ready to shoot us if they could get us in their sights. I really just gave up. As I said then, I wouldn't say I was so afraid, as that I had yielded to the real possibility of the inevitability of death. I really had concluded that day in Philadelphia, Mississippi, that it was all over. When I look back, I can find a kind of humor in the situation that was awfully difficult to see then. But we had stopped to speak and pray, and I gave a few words, saying that the murderers of the three civil rights workers who had gone to Mississippi to work, Chaney, Schwerner and Goodman, were probably around us somewhere. And all of a sudden, my speech was interrupted by a man standing behind me who said, "You damn right, I'm right behind you." I just knew my life was over, because I could tell that he wasn't bluffing at all. And when it was time to pray, Ralph Abernathy said he kept his eyes open as he spoke to God. We had a good chuckle about that later.

QUESTION: Some people who've heard it think that the speech you gave on April 3rd, 1968, before an audience of striking sanitation workers and their allies at Mason Temple in Memphis, Tennessee, contained a strong sense of premonition of death. It's not one of your better known speeches, and the only reason I bring it up is because scholars who've studied the civil rights movement and your life suggest that it might have become one of your best known speeches had you been killed that night, or shortly afterward. In retrospect, it does tend to read as a last will and testament. Did you think you would be murdered soon after you delivered that speech?

KING: Well, as I've said, death was our constant companion in the movement, and I was having an especially tough time of it. The first demonstration on behalf of the striking workers in Memphis in late March had turned violent, and there was rioting; a young black man was shot and killed. I was extremely depressed. Then the Poor People's Campaign was not going very well either. I was wearing myself out, ruining my health, really, ripping and running from one side of the country to the other trying to drum up support for our mass mobilization in Washington, D.C. My own SCLC board was against me, especially our wonderful benefactor Marian Logan, the fiery and brilliant wife of the renowned physician Arthur Logan, with whom I had many heated disagreements about the direction of our group in 1968.

On top of all that, when I was flying into Memphis to lead the march, the pilot announced, before we took off, yet another bomb threat because I was flying on the plane. Of course this kind of thing had by then become routine, but I must say to you, the thought of being killed never gets old or routine. There's an insistent, and troubling, freshness to each new threat, as if the possibility of being snuffed out renews in one's spirit a deep sense of one's fragility and finitude. I beat the feeling back, or at least I tried to, but when we landed in Memphis, there was a horrible downpour, and tornadoes in the area had already killed several people. The bleak weather seemed to match my dampened spirit, and I retreated to the Lorraine motel to get some rest, since I didn't feel very well. I sent Ralph over to the Mason Temple to speak in my place at the rally that night. Ralph rang the room and insisted I get right over because it was, how did he frame it, a Martin moment. I got dressed as fast as I could and rushed over to Mason Temple.

What you and the folk who were there that night probably heard was my fatigue, my despair, my depression, my feeling out of sorts. All of that came gurgling to the surface, I suppose, when I spoke. I can't honestly say I had any more a sense of my impending end that night than on many other nights when I felt that I could die at any moment because of the actions of our sick white brothers. In fact, I was much more convinced of my death in Philadelphia, Mississippi, in 1964 than on that night in Memphis. By the way, it turns out that the man who shouted his warning was Neshoba County Sherrif Rainey, who was allegedly implicated in the murders of those young men along with his deputy, Cecil Price. Sick brothers indeed.

QUESTION: Since you've already mentioned it, can you speak to us a bit about your depression? You were one of the most famous black people ever to publicly acknowledge that you've struggled with depression, a subject that's not often spoken about since mental health remains a big taboo in black circles.

KING: Certainly. Although I know some who read this may think I'm grossly exaggerating, I consider the announcement of my struggles with depression nearly two decades ago every bit as important in the psychological realm as breaking my silence about my opposition to the Vietnam War in 1967 was in the political realm. I decided to break my silence about my depression so that I could encourage more of our people to own up to the enormous psychic burden and emotional stress that we too often carry around. And it can have a horrible impact on our overall health. Black people have been shouldering the weight of the world, and it tells on our physical and mental health. I figured that if I told the truth, perhaps a few others might be heartened in their own struggles, and encouraged to confront what we now know is an illness that is just as much biological and physical as anything else. There should be no shame in addressing the profoundly dispiriting emotions that sometimes seize us.

I began experiencing severe bouts of depression in Montgomery during the bus boycott, when the pressures and anxiety were building at such a fast pace, and I had to call on every spiritual resource I had. I remember once I was on the podium about to speak at a mass meeting, when a wave of deep emotional suffering washed over me so strongly that I couldn't continue. My own ego and my sense of male pride kicked in, and later, when folk started saying I nearly passed out and had a small emotional breakdown, I denied it, but I eventually confessed that it was true. Of course that's not something that's easy to admit for any of us, especially for men, but I felt I had to tell the whole truth of my own battles with depression, because I'd sought the same way out—through excessive drinking and other habits of which I'm not proud—that many others have taken. But it ultimately doesn't work. Oh, it may narcotize you for a while, but it doesn't address the underlying causes of depression, which range from the chemistry of the brain, to deep psychological suffering that comes from enduring different traumas, to the stress and strain of our professions and personal lives.

Remember, I started in the movement as a very young man of 26 years of age, and by the time I was in my early 30s, I'd already confronted a huge degree of pain and suffering as a result of our push to destroy Jim Crow and institutional racism in the south. When I look back, I see it even invaded my language. I spoke in Chicago one night of how tired I was. And I . . .

QUESTION: I don't mean to interrupt you Dr. King, but it's very interesting that you mention that speech, because I had pulled it out so I could quote some of its poignant phrases to you, and ask you about them. Here are a few. "I don't mind saying to Chicago or anybody, I'm tired of marching for something that should have been mine at birth. I don't mind saying this to you this night . . . I'm tired of the tensions surrounding the days. I don't mind saying to you tonight that I'm tired of living every day under the threat of death . . . Yes, I'm tired of going to jail; I'm tired of all of the surging murmur of life's restless sea." I mean, those are remarkably direct and powerful expressions of the troubling emotions you were con-

fronting. The imagery of your suffering is simply
haunting.

KING: Yes, I suppose I felt, as sociologist Max Weber called
it, "world weary." I think that as much as I was trying to
inspire the troops to keep pushing in the war to win
America's bitter battle with itself over whether it would
do the right thing by Negroes—I mean black people; I
still revert back to the language of that era from time
to time, it just sneaks up on me, the old ways, the old
phrases, just slip right in. But as I was saying, while trying to lead our people in the fight for equality, I also
found myself fighting the gloominess of spirit that sometimes sunk me quite low. I had a number of physical and
psychological battles.

First, I often had horrible hiccups when I got anxious
or depressed, and they simply wouldn't go away—until,
miraculously enough, it was time for me to speak. Then I
could get up and deliver a speech that had no trace of a hic-
cup, but then, as soon as I was finished, they'd come right
back on me. I have no way of explaining it except to tell
you that, as I used to hear the old saints say, "God's grace
is truly sufficient." Then I'd overeat. Even though one of
my great sins, as I've always said, is eating good food,
especially soul food, when I was depressed I was nearly
eating myself into an early grave. It was quite unhealthy.
I even remember Andy Young telling me once, "Martin,
it looks like we might live through this revolution, and if

we're going to be around, we might as well be healthy." But I kept piling my plate higher and higher, and as a result, I became extremely overweight, and had to go on a serious diet to get my weight under control, although I still battle with it to this day.

From a psychological standpoint, I had such gloomy days that sometimes I just couldn't rouse myself out of bed. A couple of my aides in the sixties—long before it became even remotely acceptable to visit a therapist among the masses of Americans, much less black folk— strongly hinted that I needed to see a psychologist or a psychiatrist. My mood swings were getting progressively worse, except there wasn't much of a bi-polar manic depression going on, since I was stuck for very long periods in the depression side of that equation. I finally sought out a very smart and compassionate therapist who helped to guide me through the haze of mental injury to a healthy psychological state where I could come to grips with my wounds and bruises and recover enough to be an even more effective leader.

QUESTION: Wow, that's truly amazing. But that's not the only thing you've bravely broken your silence about. You also announced your support for the lesbian, gay, bisexual and transgender community. You even spoke at a huge rally they held in Washington, D.C., last year to oppose amending the Constitution to ban gay marriage. What led you to such an unpopular position, especially as an ordained Baptist minister?

KING: Well I said a long time ago that injustice anywhere is a threat to justice everywhere. I could not in good conscience refuse to weigh in on such a gross injustice to a precious group of God's children, our lesbian, gay, bisexual and transgender brothers and sisters. I find it abhorrent that President Bush would try to bully the country into adopting a vicious and narrow view of the Constitution by trying to use it to define marriage in such a traditional and conservative fashion. This certainly reminded me of those vicious white supremacists in the 50s and 60s who used the law and religion—and racial customs and cultural traditions—to justify their evil assaults on black folk. Now the same reactionary forces are trying to deny to sexual minorities the right to say "I do" as they see fit. It strikes me as extremely hypocritical that conservatives, who claim they want a limited government, want to expand the power of the state to tell citizens what they can do in their bedrooms.

And then the religious side of this business is quite disturbing to me as well. The same white evangelical Christians who are crusading against the rights of gays and lesbians are often descended, theologically speaking, from the very Christians who opposed us during the heyday of the civil rights movement. They pointed in their bibles to those passages that admonished the slave to obey his master; they justified segregation and racial discrimination based on twisted readings of the bible and religious history.

I'm afraid black Christians haven't done much better. The homophobia in black religious circles is so thick you could cut it with a knife. I try to challenge black clergy and laypeople alike with the message of Jesus' love for all people. There is no asterisk in the bible when Jesus brilliantly boils down the majestic sweep of the law and prophets to two central commandments: to love God with all of your heart, soul and mind, and the second one, to love your neighbor as yourself. And many black Christians seem to have no sense of either irony or history when they trot out biblical justifications for why they are opposed to homosexuality in the same manner conservative white Christians used the bible against them.

I'm ashamed to say that in the sixties I felt I had no choice but to get rid of my trusted advisor Bayard Rustin because of the vicious politics played by Adam Clayton Powell. The powerful congressman had threatened to lie and say that Rustin and I were lovers if I didn't discourage Bayard from leading a protest at the Democratic convention over the party's failure to aggressively support civil rights. It wasn't one of my shining moments of standing up for truth and righteousness. I let Adam bully me into firing a man whose strategic brilliance was unquestionable, all because of the poisonous politics of homophobia.

I have since seen the errors of my way, and I hope that we as a people, and as a nation, can welcome our gay and lesbian brothers and sisters in all aspects of our culture and nation.

QUESTION: Since we're on the topic of the black church, do you care to comment on the so-called "prosperity gospel" movement?

KING: Quite frankly, the prosperity gospel movement is a tragic development within the Christian church in general, but especially for the black church. I've never romanticized the black church; even during the height of our movement in the sixties, we never had more than a small percentage of its leadership involved. Most of the ministers in the black church and their members, I'm sorry to say, were bystanders, spectators and observers of our movement—and sometimes, they were even critical or hostile to our movement. There are a variety of reasons for such actions; black people were deathly afraid of white supremacists, and that's quite understandable. Others were bitten by the bug of otherworldly religiosity, and as I used to say about the white church, they mouthed pious irrelevancies and sanctimonious trivialities. I'm afraid the prosperity gospel has taken this trend a step further into dangerous ground. Whenever you reduce the gospel promise of freedom and liberation from oppression, and make it essentially about finding and exploiting wealth, you have perverted the meaning and intent of Jesus. I realize those are strong words, but that's simply how strongly I feel about the direction large quarters of the black church have taken by adopting the prosperity gospel perspective.

The question we must relentlessly pursue in judging the effectiveness of our religion is who are we helping and how does this serve God to bring about the transformation of the lives of the vulnerable and the forsaken. The carrot of a payoff for service in the Kingdom may drive a great many of our people to tithe or participate in the cloistered rituals of sanctuary bound politics, but it won't nudge them to actively resist economic oppression or contribute to the lives of the least fortunate. I'm terribly disturbed by how much ground we've lost in the black church to this brand of the gospel—and here I don't think we can take the metaphor lightly, because the gospel has been virtually turned into a commodity, into a designer religion which places being fashionable and trendy above the enduring concerns of sacrificing for and fighting for the poorest members of our community. The prosperity gospel movement sells the gospel at a cost, and turns a fetish with capitalism into a full-blown religious experience. The high priests of dollarism have muted the prophetic and revolutionary accents of the black Christian message of liberation and freedom and turned the sanctuary over to the money changers that Jesus drove from the temple.

QUESTION: Wow, those are strong words from you Dr. King. In light of your statement then, what do you make of the recent criticisms of prominent black figures of the black poor?

KING: Just as I am disappointed by the prosperity gospel movement, I'm equally disturbed by well-known black people and other celebrities beating up on vulnerable poor black folk. I have spent the bulk of my public career now addressing the systematic exploitation of the poor all over the world, and of course, concentrating on the American poor, especially the black and brown poor. There are horrible economic and social burdens that poor black people carry. As I've said time and time again, the civil rights movement did a great job of opening the doors for the black elite and the black middle class. The civil rights act and the voting rights act were marvelous pieces of legislation that enacted freedoms for black people who could afford to take advantage of them. Now of course all black people can, and ought to, vote. And all black people can enjoy the freedom from Jim Crow restrictions, but if we're honest with ourselves, the civil rights movement in the sixties primarily helped out those black people who could take advantage of the new opportunities we helped to make available.

But the nagging persistence of poverty for one-fourth of the black community is a staggering blight on the record of our movement, most especially on the failure of our government and society to address their plight. It does precious little good for prominent black people to

take aim at the black poor, especially when the problems
that make black people poor can't be solved by the moral-
istic recommendations that some of these figures offer. For
example, as a Baptist preacher, I'm all for black folk of
every economic strata behaving properly. I have always
preached the discipline of nonviolence, which holds dear
the notion that folk must ethically purge themselves in
order to concentrate on redemptive social action. Good
personal behavior has always been an ally in the fight
against racism because of the punishing double standard
that the Negro, I'm sorry, that black folk, have faced when
trying to make public arguments about black advance-
ment. It was exceedingly hypocritical for many of our
white brothers and sisters to hold black people to a standard that they weren't willing themselves to uphold.

I'm afraid that the hypocrisy that many of our white
brothers and sisters have given up has been transferred on
to the upper black middle class, and the black elite. Too
many well-to-do-black folk hide behind the safe security
of class status and bourgeois values and look down their
noses at the unwashed black poor, and yet they—and
really I should say we—have moral shortcomings of our
own. So it simply does no good to divide the world by
class when examining the question of moral excellence; as
I said in an essay I wrote when I was barely nineteen, some
of the smartest white people during the height of Jim
Crow were also the most racist. And some of the most
well-to-do black folk are also some of the most morally

judgmental and, quite frankly, some of the most hypocritical members of our race.

And listen, I'm not trying to be either hostile to the black elite, or celebratory of factions of the black poor who struggle with horrible habits. But the crushing circumstances of poverty that lead to all manner of social ills have barely been scoffed at, let alone strongly resisted or criticized, by the black elite. If I saw the same people who are harshly critical of the black poor make equally harsh statements about the social barriers that prevent the black poor from advancing—or if I saw them just as vigorously take to task the white brothers and sisters whose personal and corporate interests are masked behind the maintenance of black poverty and social and economic inequality—then I'd be much more inclined to see their judgment of the black poor as moral and intellectual consistency. As it stands now, their words ring rather hollow when they have not taken the time to critically analyze the complex factors that shape human behavior and that leave the poor vulnerable the world over.

QUESTION: One of the major criticisms of the black poor made by the black elite, and the black middle-class, and even a lot of working class black people, is that the family structure of the black poor, especially soaring rates of teen pregnancy leading to single female headed households, which the poor themselves can control, makes them more vulnerable to the social ills they confront.

KING: There's little doubt that we have to do a better job at family planning among the poor. I made this argument in an address that Mrs. King delivered for me on May 5, 1965, at the National Conference on Family Planning. Margaret Sanger, as you know, was at one time quite controversial because she went up against hostile cultural forces that opposed family planning as the instrument of evil, especially when it recommended birth control and later, when women gained the right of choice around the volatile issue of abortion. We must surely encourage the poor to do a better job of taking care of the homestead, and of making healthy decisions that don't unduly tax their families or overburden their resources.

But neither can I pretend that the major burden for the plight of the black family falls on the poor themselves. What we have done is basically moralize what is essentially an economic and political question. By demonizing the black poor as somehow ethically incompetent in the choices they make, we relieve the state of its responsibilities toward the poor. We make little black girls the worst offenders of the morals of society—though that is hardly the case when we examine the malfeasance that happens at the top levels of this society and government every day—and let off the hook all those who perpetuate crimes against the poor in the name of fiscal conservatism, family values and social virtue. The harsh and punitive social policies of Republican administrations over the last two decades has done more to harm the black poor family than anything any "Shaniqua" could do to harm herself.

I'm not saying that poor black girls don't need to be taught a more productive and healthy way to conduct themselves, but I'm also saying that policies of our government bear an even greater burden in the responsibility equation. And I shouldn't just speak of Republican administrations. President Bill Clinton did an awful thing when he signed the legislation for welfare reform. I personally lobbied him to think very carefully while weighing the competing interests of a conservative hegemony that was exercising tremendous political influence and the needs of the black poor who hardly had advocates in high places. Again, this is why I am personally depressed that the black elite work so vigilantly against the black poor in the name of "cleaning up" and "policing" our community morally, when they did little to nothing with their celebrity, fame and influence to lobby government and political leaders to do the right thing by the black poor. In that sense, the black elite who remained silent while the black poor were led to the political slaughter have blood on our hands too.

And in the end, let's be even more honest: there are few of us who can stand up in public and say we've never made a mistake, or done the wrong thing in a time of passion or desperation, so we should go just a bit easier on the poor who have even less of a social cushion and cultural comfort to absorb their mistakes.

QUESTION: Speaking of the conservative hegemony, what do you make of this war in Iraq and the so-called war on terror that the president has been prosecuting?

KING: It seems to me that we're heading way in the wrong direction. Let me say immediately and unequivocally that I have been saddened by the way stigma has been heaped on the heads of our Muslim brothers and sisters around the world, but especially in our country. While I stand opposed to any religious expression or justification of violence, I know that most brothers and sisters who follow Islam want peace, and love truth and justice just as much as the rest of us. I also know that the terrorists that we were concerned about for much of our history as a people bowed their knees to Jesus, not Allah. They burned the religious symbol of the cross on our lawns, and into the American collective unconscious. They dressed in cowards' garb when they donned white sheets to purify their dastardly and evil deeds. They hid behind God's name to wreak havoc and terror on black people through lynching, castration, rape and social and political intimidation. So when I think of terror, I don't think first of Al Qaeda; I think of the Ku Klux Klan and other white hate groups that have perverted and recruited a warped Christian theology in the service of truth.

As for the war in Iraq, I think it is on par with Vietnam as a tragic misuse of American might and a misled campaign to end terror when we have merely helped light a torch for terror in the minds and hearts of millions who perceive us as unjust in our exercise of power. When I called America the greatest purveyor of violence in the world in the sixties because of our involvement in Vietnam, I was accused of being unpatriotic. The rest of the country eventually caught up to my stance on that issue, it's safe to say. But the seeds of violence and empire we then sowed halfway cross the world have germinated in the soil of people in the Middle East who have felt for a long time the pressures of American empire. Let me be clear: I do not at all condone the terrorist activity of any group, for any reason, under any circumstances, even as I understand a people's or country's desperation to be released from the yoke of visible and invisible oppressions. If America is going to successfully fight terror, it must do what black folk who were fighting terror in the sixties did: we purged ourselves morally; we examined our own habits to make sure we weren't contributing unnecessarily to violence; we sought divine leadership in our pursuit of truth and justice; and we appealed to the consciences of our oppressors, while refusing to demonize them in the process of demanding fair treatment before the law. America is dealing with a dangerous threat to her borders, but she must never capitulate to blind violence and wholesale demonizing of people who have felt the crushing blows of the despotic American will across time. Since most Americans are ignorant of the tragic consequences of our foreign policy, the hatred we face as a nation comes as a surprise.

But in fighting terror, we must also fight the impulse to be self-righteous and arrogant; we should practice a bit more humility, which might go a far longer distance in getting the sort of justice and balance and security we need—and that we need to guarantee for others as well.

QUESTION: I know we're running out of time, but your quick take on three subjects: hip hop, Barack and Oprah!

KING: My goodness, what a magnificent trio of issues. Of course, I am quite critical of the violence and misogyny at the heart of so much rap music. I oppose violence in all forms, and I can't offer rap music a pass because it's made by black youth, mostly in our urban centers. But the terrible pain I face in listening to the misogyny in rap is that it is the child of our neglect as older, wiser black people. I remember once when a young lady was brought to the SCLC, complaining of being fairly ravaged by a staffer, and the men gathered there, including me, I'm ashamed to say, were cruelly insensitive to her complaints. We men have been nurtured in a male supremacist society where the needs and claims of women are at best marginal. I was a chauvinist to my wife for many, many years, and it caused a great deal of strain in our relationship, until I had to finally admit that my ways had to be reformed. It was a difficult process, and I suppose you could say I'm a recovering male supremacist. It's hard to see yourself as an oppressor on gender when you've been oppressed by race, but it's a truth we've got to face nonetheless.

That's not to say I don't like rap music; in fact, aside
from its vicious sexism and misogyny—and these are
words we had no idea about when we fought racism in the
sixties—I like the powerful stories and incredible lyrical
genius of some of the young folk in rap music. I think at
their best they have done what the black pulpit has too
many times relinquished doing: telling the ugly truth
about painful realities that demand brutal honesty in cor-
recting. And if we can forgive sexist, lecherous preachers
for their sexual sins—and you can include me in that
number, unfortunately—then we can certainly hold our
youth accountable while not doing it from a vague,
abstract sense of superior morality that won't stand up
under even the slightest scrutiny.

As for Barack Obama, I think he's a wonder of nature.
I said in the sixties that we hadn't yet produced in black
circles a political personality that had the magnetism and
respect of John F. Kennedy. I think we may have found
that person in Senator Obama. He is incredibly well-
prepared, very bright, very thoughtful, and not full of
bombast—though by nature, every politician has to brag
about what he or she has done, or will do, to lead the
country. The thought of having such a worthy person in
the highest office is simply wonderful. And the sheer
charisma and magnetism that he brings revives a sense of
expectation and hope in the electorate, and that's a stunning thing to witness coming from a black man whose
people in the South couldn't even vote for the most part

until the mid-sixties. I do caution people, however, in expecting too much from Senator Obama should he become president. A black president won't stop black suffering, but he can use his bully pulpit to speak out on social issues that matter to us, and he can help enact legislation that will address our most pressing needs—like universal healthcare, tax cuts for the poorest and neediest, not the richest Americans, and jobs and boosted wages for the working class and poor. But the need for prophets outside the system won't disappear with a black president. We must hold him accountable just as we would any other president. Now that would be a sign of real racial progress: to witness a black president engaged in his duties while facing serious scrutiny by prophetic black voices in the culture.

Finally, I am the world's biggest fan of Oprah Winfrey. I think she is a stunning figure, a woman who best represents our people's magnificent spiritual genius. Oprah's show, and her sparkling, luminous presence in the world, has done more good than a million sermons and acts of Congress. Her will to better the American people by offering an alternative to smut media is remarkable and courageous. Her support for the black poor in this country when it wasn't even popular has been stirring. Her loving embrace of our brothers and sisters in Africa has been nothing short of miraculous. She is the symbol of our will to survival through the word and spirit translated into therapeutic doses of information and transformed moral habits that provide her the most powerful pulpit in the world today. I applaud her sterling and impeccable sense of conscience, and her refusal to do anything to tarnish the black moral treasury and integrity with which she has been endowed. She has proved that white America can listen to a black voice that resonates with pure love and extraordinary compassion for the ordinary human being. I must say, I love Oprah.

# ACKNOWLEDGMENTS

In a book about the impact of death, it is only natural to think of those who have passed on, and foremost in my mind is my beloved late editor Liz Maguire, whom I miss dearly. I'd like to thank the good folk at Basic Civitas, including David Steinberger and John Sherer for seeing this book through to completion, and to Chris Greenberg for his great work over the years, and at the beginning of this book. I reserve special thanks for Amy Scheibe, a supremely gifted editor, stylist, and intellectual whose contributions made this book much better. I also have special thanks for Christine Marra, for yet another great job under impossible conditions—delivered with her trademark grace and calm under pressure. Without Amy and Christine this book wouldn't be in your hands right now.

I also thank the wonderful folk at the Martin Luther King, Jr., Center for Nonviolent Social Change, Inc. King Library and Archives in Atlanta, including the generous president and CEO Isaac Newton Farris, who graciously accommodated my last minute request and opened to me the treasure trove of the King Papers. I'm thankful as well to Cynthia Patterson Lewis, the superb archivist who along with Elaine Hall led me through the papers to find what I needed with a beautiful smile and a lovely spirit.

I am grateful to my colleagues at Georgetown, my new academic home, especially President John DeGioia and Provost James O'Donnell, two shining stars in the academic firmament whose leadership is uplifting. And I thank Derreck Brown for his incredibly expert help and his efficient handling of business. I also thank Kirby Blem and Harrison Lyle Beacher for their wonderful help. I'd also like to thank the fine students at Georgetown who helped with library research of articles and books, including Michael Moore (who graciously and efficiently coordinated his fellow students) and Ashley Bowen, Graham Eng-Wilmot, Pamela Nwaoko, Kate Morrissey, Lisa McDowell (who provided crucial assistance), LiAnna Davis, Gillian Brooks, and Monica Anderson.

I thank as usual my cadre of friends who offer love, wisdom and insight: Susan "Queen" Taylor and Khephra "Smooth" Burns; Stan and Barbara Perkins; Andriette and Khaska; Yolanda and Horace (thanks for picking up my American Book Award and delivering my remarks, and for all that great music); to Linda Johnson Rice and Mel Farr; Michelle Miller and Marc Morial; Karen Lloyd; and of course to Soyini.

I'm grateful as always to my wonderful family—my mother Addie Mae Dyson, and my brothers Anthony,

Everett, Gregory and Brian; my cousin Oscar Madison; and my children, Michael II, Cory and Maisha (God bless your child), and Mwata. And finally, to Rev. Marcia Louise Dyson for her brilliant mind, and for her dedicated service to humanity.

# BIBLIOGRAPHICAL NOTES

The majority of quotes from Martin Luther King in this book
come from the papers of Dr. King housed in the Martin Luther
King Center for Nonviolent Social Change, Inc. King Library
and Archives in Atlanta; collections of his sermons derived
from the monumental Martin Luther King, Jr., Papers Project
at Stanford University and the King Center in Atlanta, edited
by Clayborne Carson; the major single volume collection of his
writings, edited by James Washington; and major biographical
and intellectual studies of King. These include Clayborne Carson, editor, *A Knock at Midnight: Inspiration from the Great Sermons of Reverend Martin Luther King, Jr.* (New York: Warner
Books, 1998) and *A Call to Conscience: The Landmark Speeches of
Dr. Martin Luther King, Jr.* (New York: Warner Books, 2001);
James M. Washington, editor, *A Testament of Hope: The Essential
Writings and Speeches of Martin Luther King, Jr.* (New York:
HarperCollins, 1986) and *I Have a Dream: Writings and Speeches
That Changed the World* (New York: HarperCollins, 1992);
David Garrow, *Bearing the Cross: Martin Luther King, Jr., and the
Southern Christian Leadership Conference* (New York: William
Morrow, 1986); Taylor Branch's trilogy, *Parting the Waters:
America in the King Years, 1954–63* (New York: Simon and
Schuster, 1988); *Pillar of Fire: America in the King Years,*

*1963–65* (New York: Simon and Schuster, 1998), and *At Canaan's Edge: America in the King Years, 1965–68* (New York: Simon & Schuster, 2006); and Michael Eric Dyson, *I May Not Get There with You: The True Martin Luther King, Jr.* (New York: Free Press, 2000).

Following are the bibliographical sources of quotes and statistics and references for each chapter.

## CHAPTER 1

"King Urges Black Muslims Stand Together in Peace," *Chicago Defender*, March 1, 1965, pp. 1, 10.

Coretta Scott King, *My Life with Martin Luther King, Jr.* (New York: Holt, Rinehart, 1969).

## CHAPTER 2

I coined the term automortology from a combination of autothanatography, used by theorists like Jacques Derrida, Louis Marin, and Maurice Blanchot; autothanatology, used by Ivan Callus; and automortography, used by Thomas H. Kane. Interestingly, Kane, neither in his article on Martin Luther King, Jr., nor in the dissertation from which it is drawn, cites none of the literature on autothanatology/autothanatography, even though it clearly establishes an intellectual precedent for his conception of automortography. I prefer automortology rather than automortography when discussing King since it underscores the spoken word and not the written text, a difference of *ology* (as in logos, or word, or speech) and *graphy* (writing). See Jacques Derrida, *The Post Card: From Socrates to Freud and Beyond,* trans. Alan Bass (Chicago: University of Chicago, 1986); Ivan Callus, "(Auto)Thanatography or (Auto)Thanatology? Mark C. Taylor, Simon Critchley and the Writing of the Dead," *Forum for Modern Language Studies* 41, no. 4 (2005): 427–438; and Thomas H. Kane, "Mourning the Promised Land: Martin Luther King Jr.'s Automortography and the National Civil Rights Museum," *American Literature* 76, no. 3 (September 2004), and his dissertation, *Last Acts: Automortography and the Cultural Performance of Death in the United States, 1968–2001,* University of Virginia, 2003.

John Murphy, "Inventing Authority: Bill Clinton, Martin Luther King, Jr., and the Orchestration of Rhetorical Traditions," *Quarterly Journal of Speech* 83, no. 1 (February 1997): 71–89.

Thomas Rosteck, "Narrative in Martin Luther King's *I've Been to the Mountaintop,*" *The Southern Communication Journal* 58 (Fall 1992): 1.

## CHAPTER 3

William Brink and Louis Harris, *Black and White: A Study of U.S. Racial Attitudes Today* (New York: Simon and Schuster, 1966).

Michael Eric Dyson, *Holler If You Hear Me: Searching for Tupac Shakur* (New York: Basic Civitas, 2001).

Christine Harold and Kevin Michael DeLuca, "Behold the Corpse: Violent Images and the Case of Emmett Till," *Rhetoric & Public Affairs* 8, no. 2 (2005): 263–286.

Rodney T. Hartnett and Carol U. Libby, "Agreement with

Views of Martin Luther King, Jr. before and after His Assassination," *Phylon* 33, no. 1 (1st Qtr. 1972): 79–87.

C. Richard Hofstetter, "Political Disengagement and the Death of Martin Luther King," *The Public Opinion Quarterly* 33, no. 2 (Summer 1969): 174–179.

James Peterson, "'Dead Prezence': Money and Mortal Themes in Hip Hop Culture," *Callaloo* 29, no. 3 (2006): 895–909.

Leonard Shengold, *Soul Murder: The Effects of Childhood Abuse and Deprivation* (New Haven: Yale University Press, 1989).

Andrew Young, *An Easy Burden: The Civil Rights Movement and the Transformation of America* (New York: HarperCollins, 1996).

## CHAPTER 4

*Bureau of Justice Statistics,* http://www.ojp.usdoj.gov/bjs/pub/pdf/bvvc.pdf.

William Jefferson Clinton, "Memphis Church of God in Christ Church Address," http://www.americanrhetoric.com/speeches/wjclintonmemphis.htm.

Department of Justice Statistics, http://www.ojp.usdoj.gov/bjs/pub/pdf/pjim06.pdf.

Economic Mobility of Black and White Families, http://www.economicmobility.org/assets/pdfs/EMP_Black_White_Families.pdf.

PEW-Economic Mobility Project, http//www.economicmobility.org/reports_and_research/Economic%20Mobility%20Project%20Fact%20Sheet.pdf.

Amaad Rivera, Brenda Cotto-Escalera, Anisha Desai, Jeannette Huezo, and Dedrick Muhammad (Institute for Policy

Studies), *Foreclosed: State of the Dream 2008,* http://www.faireconomy.org/files/pdf/StateOfDream_01_16_08_Web.pdf.

U.S. Census Bureau Current Population Report, "Income, Poverty, and Health Insurance Coverage in the United States 2006," http://www.census.gov/prod/2007pubs/p60-233.pdf.

———, http://www.census.gov/population/www/socdemo/race/ppl-186.html.

———, http://www.census.gov/population/socdemo/race/black/ppl-186/tab13a.html.

U.S. Department of Education, National Center for Education Statistics, http://nces.ed.gov/programs/digest/d06/tables_1.asp#Ch1Sub5.

———, http://nces.ed.gov/programs/digest/d06/tables/dt06_019.asp?referrer=list.

United States Sentencing Committee 2007, http://www.ussc.gov/r_congress/cocaine2007.pdf.

## CHAPTER 5

Bill Clinton, *My Life* (New York: Knopf, 2004).

Herbert Gutman, *The Black Family in Slavery and Freedom, 1750–1925* (New York: Pantheon, 1976).

## CHAPTER 6

Ralph David Abernathy, *And the Walls Came Tumbling Down: An Autobiography* (New York: Harper & Row, 1989).

Michael K. Honey, *Going Down Jericho Road: The Memphis Strike,*

*Martin Luther King's Last Campaign* (New York: Norton, 2007).

Thomas F. Jackson, *From Civil Rights to Human Rights: Martin Luther King, Jr., and the Struggle for Economic Justice* (Philadelphia: University of Pennsylvania Press, 2007).

## CHAPTER 7

John Lewis, *Walking with the Wind: A Memoir of the Movement* (New York: Simon and Schuster, 1998).

Richard Lischer, *The Preacher King: Martin Luther King, Jr. and the Word that Moved America* (New York: Oxford University Press, 1995).

## CHAPTER 8

Marshall Frady, *Jesse: The Life and Pilgrimage of Jesse Jackson* (New York: Random House, 1996).

Jesse Jackson, Roger D. Hatch, and Frank E. Watkins, *Straight from the Heart* (Minneapolis: Fortress Press, 1987).

Jesse Jackson and Charles Murray, "What Does the Government Owe the Poor? Welfare, Race, and the Wealth of a Nation," *Harper's Magazine,* April 1986.

Arthur Kretchmer, "Jesse Jackson: A Candid Conversation with the Fiery Heir Apparent to Martin Luther King," *Playboy*, November 1969.

Richard Levine, "Jesse Jackson: Heir to Dr. King?" *Harper's Magazine,* March 1969.

Barbara Reynolds, *Jesse Jackson: America's David* (Washington, D.C.: JFJ Associates, 1985 [1975]).

John Alfred Williams, *The King God Didn't Save: Reflections on the Life and Death of Martin Luther King, Jr.* (New York: Coward-McCann, Inc., 1970).

## CHAPTER 9

Wayne Barrett, "What Al Did to Jesse: Sharpton and Jackson: 'They were kind of the best of enemies,'" *Village Voice,* December 7, 2004.

——, "On a New High, Sharpton Hits a New Low: TV's Democratic minister of 'moral' values take a hypocritical plunge," *Village Voice,* December 7, 2004.

Robin D. G. Kelley, *Race Rebels: Culture, Politics, and the Black Working Class* (New York: Free Press, 1994).

Al Sharpton with Karen Hunter, *Al on America* (New York: Kensington Books, 2002).

Al Sharpton and Anthony Walton, *"Go and Tell Pharaoh": The Autobiography of the Reverend Al Sharpton* (New York: Doubleday, 1996).

Clarence Taylor, *Black Religious Intellectuals: The Fight for Equality from Jim Crow to the Twenty-First Century* (New York: Routledge, 2002).

## CHAPTER 10

Barack Obama, *Dreams from My Father: A Story of Race and Inheritance* (New York: Crown, 1995).

——, *The Audacity of Hope: Thoughts on Reclaiming the American Dream* (New York: Crown, 2006).

Remarks of Senator Barack Obama, Howard University

Convocation, Washington, D.C., September 28, 2007, http://www.barackobama.com/2007/09/28/remarks_of_ senator_barack_obam_26.php.

Frank Rich, "Next Up for the Democrats: Civil War," *New York Times*, February 10, 2008.

# INDEX